# my knitting journal

*this journal belongs to*

**CICO BOOKS**

LONDON NEW YORK

# Contents

# useful addresses and mail order

## USA

**Cascade Yarns**
www.cascadeyarns.com for
stockists.

**Classic Elite Yarns**
300A Jackson Street
Lowell
MA 01852
Tel: 978 453 2837
Fax: 978 452 3085
www.classiceliteyarns.com

**Colinette Yarns**
Unique Kolours
28 North Bacton Hill Rd
Malvern
PA 19355
Tel: 001 610 644 4885
Fax: 001 610 644 4886
www.uniquekolours.com

**Debbie Bliss, Louisa
Harding and Noro**
Knitting Fever Inc
315 Bayview Avenue
Amityville
NY 11701
Tel: 516 546 3600
Fax: 516 546 6871
www.knittingfever.com

**Filatura Di Crosa and
Tahki**
Tahki Stacy Charles, Inc.
Building 36
70-30 80th Street

Ridgewood
NY 11385
Tel: 800 338 yarn
www.tahkistacycharles.com

**GGH and Muench Yarns**
1323 Scott Street
Petaluma
CA 94954-1135
Tel toll-free: 800 733 9276
Tel local: 707 763 9377
Fax: 707 763 9477
www.muenchyarns.com

**Jaimeson's and
Simply Shetland**
10 Domingo Road
Santa Fe
NM 87508
www.simplyshetland.com

**Karabella Yarns**
1201 Broadway
New York
NY 10001
Tel toll-free: 800 550 0898
Tel local: 212 684 2665
Fax: 646 935 0588
www.karabellayarns.com

**Knitche**
5150 Main Street
Downers Grove
IL 60515
Tel: 630-852-5648
Fax: 630-852-5645
www.knitche.com

**Kollage Yarns**
www.kollageyarns.com for
stockists.

**Peace Fleece**
475 Porterfield Road,
Porter
Maine 04068
www.peacefleece.com

**Plymouth Yarn Co**
P.O. Box 28
Bristol
PA 19007
Tel: 215 788 0459
www.plymouthyarn.com

**Prism Yarns**
www.prismyarn.com for
stockists.

**Rowan Yarns**
Westminster Fibers Inc.
4 Townsend West
Suite 8
Nashua,
NH 03063
Tel: 603 886 5041
Fax: 603 886 1056
www.westminsterfibers.com

**Rumpelstiltskin**
1021 R Street
Sacramento
CA 95814
Tel: 916 442 9225
www.yarnyarnyarn.com

**String**
130 East 82nd Street
New York
NY 10028
Tel: 212 288 yarn
www.string yarns .com

**Strings and Strands**
5299 Roswell Rd
Suite 114
Atlanta
Georgia 30342
Tel:404.252.9662
www.stringsandstrands.com

**Wonderful Things**
232 Stockbridge Road
Great Barrington
MA 01230
Tel: 413 528 2473
Fax: 413 528 0526
www.wonderful-things.com

**Yarn Lady**
Oakbrook Village
Suite M
24371 Avenida De La
Carlota
Laguna Hills
CA 92653
Tel: Toll free 888-770-7809
Local 949 770 7809
Fax: 949 496 2432
www.yarnlady.com

**Yarnmarket**
1-888-996-9276
www.yarnmarket.com

**UK**

**Colinette Yarns**
Banwy Workshops
Llanfair Caereinion
Powys
Wales SY21 0SG
Tel: 01938 810128
Fax: 01938 810127
www.colinette.com

**Debbie Bliss, Louisa Harding and Noro**
Designer Yarns Ltd
Units 8–10 Newbridge
Industrial Estate
Pitt Street
Keighley
West Yorkshire BD21 4PQ
Tel: 01535 664222
Fax: 01535 664333
www.designeryarns.uk.com

**Loop**
41 Cross Street
Islington
London N1 2BB
Tel: 020 7288 1160
www. loop.gb.com

**Rooster Yarns**
Southover Nurseries
Spring Lane
Burwash
East Sussex TN19 7JB
Tel: 01435 884010
www.roosteryarns.com

**Rowan Yarns**
Green Lane Mill
Holmfirth
West Yorkshire HD9 2DX
Tel: 01484 681881
www.knitrowan.com

**Texere Yarns**
College Mill
Barkerend Road
Bradford BD1 4AU
Tel: 01274 722191
Fax: 01274 393500
www.texere.co.uk

**Twilleys of Stamford**
Thomas B. Ramsden
(Bradford) Limited
Netherfield Road
Guiseley
Leeds LS20 9PD
Tel: 01943 872264
Fax: 01943 878689
www.twilleys.co.uk

**INTERNATIONAL**

Adriafil Yarns
www.adriafil.com for
stockists.

Anny Blatt
www.annyblatt.com for
stockists.

Garnstudio
www.garnstudio.com for
stockists.

# favorite shops and suppliers

name:

address:


tel:

fax:

email:

www:


name:

address:


tel:

fax:

email:

www:


name:

address:


tel:

fax:

email:

www:


name:

address:


tel:

fax:

email:

www:


name:

address:


tel:

fax:

email:

www:


name:

address:


tel:

fax:

email:

www:

name:

address:

tel:

fax:

email:

www:

name:

address:

tel:

fax:

email:

www:

name:

address:

tel:

fax:

email:

www:

name:

address:

tel:

fax:

email:

www:

name:

address:

tel:

fax:

email:

www:

name:

address:

tel:

fax:

email:

www:

# favorite websites

www:

notes:

www:

notes:

www:

notes:

www:

notes:

wwww:

notes:

wwww:

notes:

www:

notes:

www:

notes:

www: ....................................................................

notes: ..................................................................

.............................................................................

.............................................................................

.............................................................................

.............................................................................

www: ....................................................................

notes: ..................................................................

.............................................................................

.............................................................................

.............................................................................

.............................................................................

wwww: ..................................................................

notes: ..................................................................

.............................................................................

.............................................................................

.............................................................................

.............................................................................

www: ....................................................................

notes: ..................................................................

.............................................................................

.............................................................................

.............................................................................

.............................................................................

www: ....................................................................

notes: ..................................................................

.............................................................................

.............................................................................

.............................................................................

.............................................................................

www: ....................................................................

notes: ..................................................................

.............................................................................

.............................................................................

.............................................................................

.............................................................................

wwww: ..................................................................

notes: ..................................................................

.............................................................................

.............................................................................

.............................................................................

.............................................................................

www: ....................................................................

notes: ..................................................................

.............................................................................

.............................................................................

.............................................................................

.............................................................................

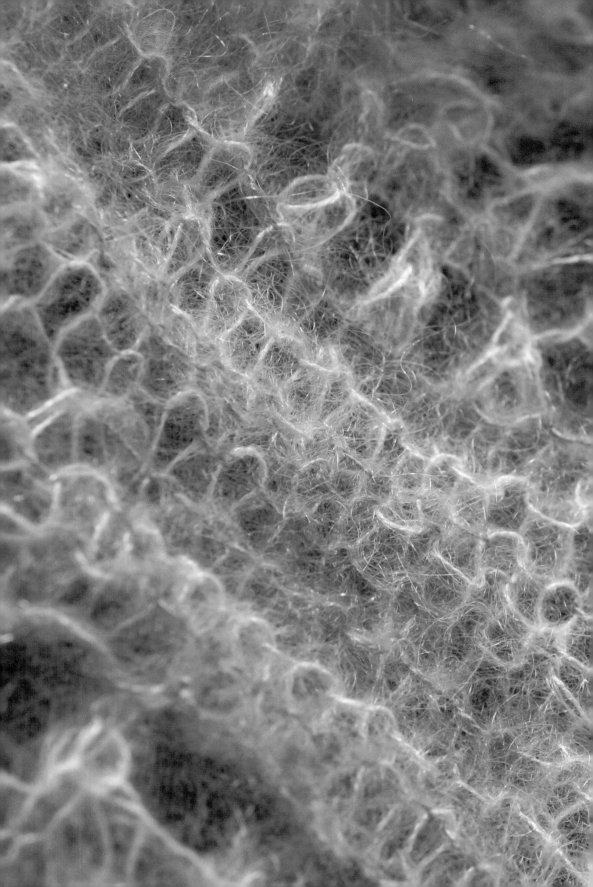

# knitting equipment

All you really need to start knitting are a pair of knitting needles and some yarn. However, as you progress you'll find you need other items to work some patterns (for example, stitch holders and round markers), and there are other items that aren't essential, but that will make some tasks easier. All the equipment shown here is readily available from craft stores and mail-order companies—you'll find some addresses at the front of this journal. Turn to page 14 for information on different types of yarn.

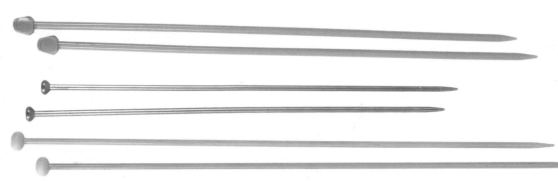

Above: knitting needles are usually made from plastic (top), metal (center), or bamboo (bottom). Choose whichever you prefer, though if you are a knitting novice you might find bamboo needles easiest, as the yarn slips along them less readily, and you are less likely to drop a stitch.

Right and below: circular needles (right), and double-pointed needles (below), are used for circular knitting. Double-pointed needles (dpn), are best for small objects such as socks and hats, while circular needles, which are available in different lengths, can be used to knit certain styles of sweaters and bags.

Left: a crochet hook, either made of metal or, as shown here, wood, is a great help in picking up dropped stitches (see page 47).

Below: cable needles come in two styles, straight (left), and cranked (right). They do exactly the same job, but a cranked needle is recommended if you are a beginner to cabling, as it will help prevent you dropping the stitches as you work the cable twist.

Right: keep a pair of small sharp scissors to hand for cutting yarn. Never try and break yarn with your hands; some types are surprisingly strong and you risk pulling and distorting the knitting, and hurting your fingers.

Above: a stiff ruler is best for measuring tension (see page 18), as it will lie flat across the knitting. Use either a metal one, as shown, or a plastic one.

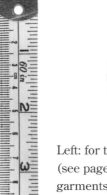

Left: for taking body measurements (see page 16) and measuring sections of garments, use a tape measure. Choose whichever measurement system you prefer, imperial or metric, but don't swap between them when working on a project.

Above: keep some small and large safety pins in your knitting bag: they are ideal for holding small numbers of stitches in the same way as specialist stitch holders (opposite).

Above: there are two types of knitting marker—position markers (left), and stitch markers (right). Position markers are placed between stitches to mark the beginning of a round in circular knitting, or an increase or decrease point in straight knitting. Stitch markers are used to mark a particular stitch that you will need to refer back to later in a pattern.

Above: when you are working color knitting, wind lengths of the yarns you are using onto separate bobbins and knit from these to avoid ending up with a horrible tangle of balls of yarn.

Above: point protectors are useful: they stop knitting sliding off the needle when you are not working on it, and they prevent the points punching holes in your knitting bag.

Above: some patterns require you to place a specified number of stitches on a holder while you work on others. The most commonly available stitch holders are like large safety pins (top), but you can get double-ended ones (below). The latter are useful as you can knit the stitches off either end of them, rather than having to place them on a needle first.

Above: a row counter is another handy item. Slip one onto a knitting needle and clock up the rows as you work to make sure you don't lose your position in a pattern.

Above: knitter's pins are thicker and blunter than dressmaker's pins so that they do not split the stitches when you pin pieces of knitting together. They also have large heads so that you can see them easily.

Right: knitter's sewing needles have blunt tips so that, like knitter's pins, they do not split the stitches when you are sewing pieces of knitting together. They come in different sizes, so choose one with an eye large enough to accommodate the yarn you are using.

# types of yarn

There are many different yarns to choose from—in fact the array can be quite bewildering. However, commercial patterns will always list a specific yarn to use. Yarns are categorized by weight, which in turn depends on the thickness and number of plies, or strands, used to spin it. Though two yarns of the same weight may vary slightly in thickness, the categories are recognized worldwide. Here is useful information on the most popular yarns.

*wool yarns* Made from the fleeces of of sheep, goats, and rabbits, wool yarns are the most popular and most commonly used by knitters all over the world. Indeed, so popular are these yarns that many people talk about "wool," even if the yarn they are referring to is made from pure cotton.

Wool is an excellent yarn to knit with, its elasticity and softness making it kind on the hands and forgiving of a beginner's rather uneven tension. However, these qualities do vary from weight to weight and brand to brand. Smooth wool yarns show stitch detail well and so are good for textured knitting, but the fluffier types will blur the stitches and are best reserved for plain knitting.

Some people, especially babies and children, find wool too itchy if worn next to the skin. If this is the case, there are a number of wool-mix yarns (wool-cotton or wool-silk) that are softer and easier to wear, while still retaining the benefits of knitting with wool. Also, today many wool yarns are machine washable, making them ideal for children's garments, though do always check the yarn ball band for washing instructions.

Above, top to bottom: mohair yarn is a lightweight, fluffy yarn made from the hair of the angora goat. Fingering/baby/4-ply yarn is lightweight and good for making items such as lacy garments and, as the name suggests, clothes and accessories for babies and children. Wool-cotton mix yarn in a sport/DK weight is a popular yarn mix that knits up well and is machine washable. Sport/DK weight yarn is ideal for garments for children and adults alike. Worsted/Aran weight yarn is probably the most commonly used weight of yarn; it is perfect for clothes and accessories. Bulky/chunky weight yarns knit up quickly and so are popular with beginners, though the larger size of needle they demand can be clumsy to handle. Extra-bulky/super-chunky is an even thicker yarn, the heaviest weight commonly available.

*cotton yarns* These are made from the seedhead of the cotton plant. Cotton yarns are cool and so ideal for summer garments, though beginners can find them tricky to work. This is because their lack of elasticity can make them a little hard on the hands and, maybe more importantly, unforgiving of wobbly tension. However, the smooth surface of cotton yarn—especially if it is mercerized, making it extra-lustrous—means that it shows stitch detail beautifully, so it is perfect for textured stitch patterns.

Cotton yarns can usually be machine-washed—though they are slow to dry—and are not itchy on the skin, making them ideal for babies, and anyone with sensitive skin.

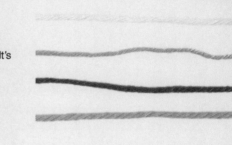

Right, top to bottom: mercerized cotton; any weight of cotton can be treated with a mercerized finish, this is a fingering/baby/4-ply weight. Denim yarn is usually only available in white, blue, and black: it shrinks and fades when first washed and should only be used with denim yarn patterns.

Fingering/baby/4-ply cotton is ideal for children's garments in both texture and weight. Sport/DK weight yarn is, like its wool counterpart, great for adult's and children's garments. Worsted/Aran weight is the heaviest weight of yarn that cotton is usually spun to.

*novelty and synthetic yarns* The revival of interest in knitting has also seen an increase in the range of novelty yarns. These are yarns that produce a textured or colored effect when knitted up. This has made them popular with beginners, as interesting effects can be created easily. However, do be cautious when using novelty yarns, sometimes the effect is surprising!

Most novelty yarns, and a wide range of plain yarns, are made from synthetic, or man-made, fibers. These yarns are washable and durable, but many knitters are not keen on the feel of the final fabric.

Left, top to bottom: hemp yarn is derived from the hemp plant and though it is cool and lightweight, it is rather stiff, making it better suited for accessories than for garments. Space-dyed, or variegated, yarns change color along their length—beware, they can knit up rather oddly. Tweed yarns have "knops" of color spun into them and can be soft and subtle, or bright and bold. Silk yarns are soft and luxurious to the touch, but can be tricky to knit as they have little elasticity. Eyelash yarn has fine fibers coming out of a central core and when knitted up has a furry finish; this particular yarn is also variegated. Ribbon yarn twists as it is knitted, resulting in a signature uneven fabric: the yarn shown here has a lurex strand for a touch of sparkle. Bouclé yarn is not the easiest for a beginner to handle, as its quite easy to push the knitting needle through the yarn rather than through the stitch loop, but it can look effective used on cuffs and collars.

# taking measurements

When you buy a pattern to knit, check that it gives the size options you need. Many patterns offer a range of sizes and will give finished garment measurements, so measure the person the garment is for, and check that the pattern gives that size. Here is a list of the most useful measurements to know and where to measure the body to establish them. Fill in the measurements of the people you usually knit for on the page opposite and you will have all the information you need when buying a new pattern.

*measuring* Use a cloth tape measure to measure the body and do not pull it too tight; a comfortable fit is what you are aiming for. Not all these measurements will be given on a knitting pattern, but use them to check the garment pieces as you knit to guarantee a perfect fit.

Bust/chest: measure around the fullest part of the torso, making sure that the tape measure doesn't slip down across the back.

Waist: measure around the narrowest part of the torso. (It's helpful to tie a piece of yarn around the waist and leave it there to mark the waistline while taking the rest of the measurements.)

Hips: measure around the fullest part, usually about 8–10in/23–25cm below the waistline (marked by a piece of yarn), making sure that the tape measure doesn't slip up or down at the back.

Back length: measure from the nape of the neck to the waist.

Back width: measure across the back, from the edge of one shoulder to the edge of the other shoulder.

One shoulder: measure from the middle of the nape of the neck to the outside edge of one shoulder.

Waist to underarm: measure from the waistline to about 1in/2.5cm below the armpit.

Inside arm length: measure from the wrist to about 1in/2.5cm before the armpit.

Center back neck to wrist: holding the arm a little out to the side, with the elbow slightly bent, measure from the middle of the nape of the neck, across the shoulder, and down around the elbow to the wrist. This measurement minus that for one shoulder will give you the sleeve length measurement.

Upper arm circumference: measure around the fullest part of the arm between the shoulder and the elbow.

Wrist circumference: measure around the wrist, just above the hand.

Head circumference: measure around the fullest part of the head, usually in line with the eyebrows. As well as being the measurement you need for a hat, this measurement is useful in knowing how wide a neckline has to be to pass easily over the head.

name:

bust/chest:

waist:

hips:

back length:

back width:

one shoulder:

waist to underarm:

inside arm length:

center back neck to wrist:

upper arm circumference:

wrist circumference:

head circumference:


name:

bust/chest:

waist:

hips:

back length:

back width:

one shoulder:

waist to underarm:

inside arm length:

center back neck to wrist:

upper arm circumference:

wrist circumference:

head circumference:


name:

bust/chest:

waist:

hips:

back length:

back width:

one shoulder:

waist to underarm:

inside arm length:

center back neck to wrist:

upper arm circumference:

wrist circumference:

head circumference:


name:

bust/chest:

waist:

hips:

back length:

back width:

one shoulder:

waist to underarm:

inside arm length:

center back neck to wrist:

upper arm circumference:

wrist circumference:

head circumference:


name:

bust/chest:

waist:

hips:

back length:

back width:

one shoulder:

waist to underarm:

inside arm length:

center back neck to wrist:

upper arm circumference:

wrist circumference:

head circumference:


name:

bust/chest:

waist:

hips:

back length:

back width:

one shoulder:

waist to underarm:

inside arm length:

center back neck to wrist:

upper arm circumference:

wrist circumference:

head circumference:

# knitting a swatch

There are two reasons for knitting a swatch; to work out your gauge/tension on a particular yarn and to see how a yarn knits up.

*knitting a gauge/tension swatch* When you buy a pattern it will specify the yarn you need to knit it and the gauge/tension required. This is the number of stitches and rows to a specific measurement, usually 4in/10cm. It is important you work to the gauge/tension the pattern asks for or the finished garment will be too big (if your tension is too loose), or too small (if your tension is too tight). So you must always knit a gauge/tension swatch, even if you have knitted another pattern in the same yarn, as tensions vary from pattern to pattern.

To knit a gauge/tension swatch, first find the tension information in the pattern. It will say something like: "22 stitches and 28 rows to 4in/10cm over stockinette/stocking stitch using US 6/4mm needles." Use the size of needles specified to cast on the number of stitches stated, plus ten. Knit the number of rows stated, plus ten, then bind/cast off.

Lay the swatch flat, without stretching it. To count the number of stitches, lay a ruler across the swatch so that 4in/10cm (or the distance stated in the pattern) is measured out a few stitches in from either edge. Put a pin into the swatch at either end of the measured distance. Remove the ruler and count the number of stitches between the pins.

To count the number of rows, repeat the process, but lay the ruler vertically on the swatch so that 4in/10cm is measured out a few rows from either edge in that direction.

It is important to measure the specified distance a few stitches or rows in from the edges, as the cast on and bound/cast off edges and the row ends can be tighter or looser than the stitches in the middle.

If you have the same number of stitches and rows as stated in the pattern, then you have the correct tension. If you have too few stitches and rows, knit the swatch again using needles one size smaller. If you have too many stitches and rows, then try again with needles one size larger. This may sound time-consuming and annoying, but it's much better to knit a little square a few times than to spend days knitting a garment that doesn't fit.

*how a yarn knits up* When you buy a new yarn—either for a particular pattern, or just because love it—it is important to know how it will look and feel when it is knitted up. This might affect what you choose to use it for and what stitch patterns will look best knitted in it.

If you are working with a yarn you have bought because you liked it, but you don't yet know what you will knit with it, then you don't have to cast on a specific number of stitches. However, do knit a swatch that is a reasonable size or you won't have enough knitted fabric to get a true idea of how the yarn knits up.

Work the swatch in stockinette/stocking stitch, as this is the most common pattern. However, if you are using an unusual yarn, such as a novelty yarn, then work a variety of stitch patterns to see how they all look. Some stitches look fine in a particular yarn, while others don't work at all.

If you are using a variegated color yarn, then ensure your swatch shows all the color changes. Though the colors will sit differently across a larger number of stitches, a good-sized swatch will give you an idea of how they will look.

If you are going to display your swatches, knit them with a seed/moss stitch border. This will help to keep them flat and give them a professional look.

Above: a swatch of variegated color yarn knitted in stockinette/stocking stitch.

Above: a swatch of lurex yarn knitted in different stitch patterns. Top to bottom: single rib, stockinette/stocking stitch, seed/moss stitch, reverse stockinette/stocking stitch, garter stitch.

Above: a stockinette/stocking stitch swatch with a seed/moss stitch border.

# *substituting yarn*

Sometimes you will find a pattern you love, but in a yarn you don't like. You can substitute another yarn, but there are some rules you must follow.

The yarn you want to use must be a similar weight to the pattern yarn. Don't use a bulky/chunky yarn if the pattern asks for a sport/DK weight or you will have problems.

The pattern will give the number of balls of yarn needed, but you can't just buy the same number of balls of your chosen yarn, as different brands, even of the same type and ball weight, can contain different quantities of

yarn. Check the yardage/meterage per ball of the pattern yarn and multiply that figure by the number of balls needed to get the total yardage/meterage needed, and buy the same yardage/meterage of your chosen yarn.

You must knit a gauge/tension swatch in your chosen yarn before you start the project. Different brands of yarn, even of the same weight, will not necessarily knit up to the same tension.

If you are substituting a yarn, choose one of a similar weight or the pattern can knit up very differently indeed.

# abbreviations

On the whole abbreviations are fairly standard across all commercial patterns, though you will find some small variations. Pattern books use variations to different degrees, though they should always list all the abbreviations used in all of the projects. Here is a list of the most commonly used standard abbreviations.

**A**
**A, B, C, etc** colors as indicated in the pattern
**alt** alternate
**approx** approximate

**B**
**bc** back cross
**beg** begin, beginning, begins
**bo** bind off

**C**
**C4B** cable four (or number stated) back
**C4F** cable four (or number stated) front
**cc** contrast color
**cm** centimeter(s)
**cn** cable needle
**co** cast on
**col** color
**cont** continue
**cr** cross
**cr l** cross left
**cr r** cross right

**D**
**dbl** double
**dec(s)** decrease, decreasing, decreases
**diam** diameter
**DK** double knitting
**dpn** double-pointed needle

**F**
**fc** front cross
**foll(s)** following, follows

**G**
**g** gram(s)
**g st** garter stitch

**I**
**in** inch(es)
**inc(s)** increase, increasing, increases
**incl** including

**K**
**k2tog** knit two together
**k2tog tbl** knit two together through the backs of the loops
**k** knit
**ktbl** knit through the back of the loop
**kfb** knit into the front and back of a stitch
**kwise** knitwise

**L**
**lc** left cross
**lh** left hand
**l(h)n** left (hand) needle
**lt** left twist

**M**
**m** meter(s)
**mb** make bobble
**ml** make loop

**mc** main color
**mm** millimeters
**M1** make one stitch

**O**
**oz** ounce(es)

**P**
**p2tog** purl two together
**p2tog tbl** purl two together through the backs of the loops
**p** purl
**patt(s)** pattern(s)
**PB** place bead
**pfb** purl into the front and back of a stitch
**pm** place marker
**pnso** pass next stitch over
**psso** pass slipped stitch over
**PS** place sequin
**ptbl** purl through the back of the loop
**pwise** purlwise

**R**
**rc** right cross
**rem** remain, remaining
**rep(s)** repeat(s)
**rev st st** reverse stockinette/stocking stitch
**rh** right hand
**r(h)n** left (hand) needle
**rnd(s)** round(s)
**RS** right side
**rt** right twist

S
**sk** skip
**skp(o)** slip one, knit one, pass
  slipped stitch over
**sl** slip
**sl st** slip stitch
**ssk** slip, slip, knit
**st(s)** stitch(es)
**st st** stockinette/stocking stitch

T
**T2B** twist two (or number
  stated) back
**T2F** twist two (or number
  stated) forward
**tbl** through the back of the loop
**tog** together

W
**WS** wrong side
**wyib** with yarn in back
**wyif** with yarn in front

Y
**yb** yarn back
**yd** yard(s)
**yf** yarn forward
**yfon** yarn forward and over
  needle
**yfrn** yarn forward and round
  needle
**yo** yarn over
**yo2(3)** yarn over twice
  (three times)
**yfrn** yarn over needle
**yrn** yarn round needle
**ytb** yarn to back
**ytf** yarn to front

**\*** repeat instructions
  between/following * as many
  times as instructed
**[ ]** repeat instructions between [ ]
  as many times as instructed

# US/UK terms

Knitters on either side of the Atlantic use slightly different terminology when it comes to knitting. This book gives US/UK terms throughout, but you may find these lists helpful when looking at other pattern books.

## knitting terms

| US | UK |
|---|---|
| baby yarn | 4-ply yarn |
| bind off | cast off |
| bulky yarn | chunky yarn |
| extra-bulky yarn | super-chunky yarn |
| fingering yarn | 4-ply yarn |
| finish (garment) | make up (garment) |
| fisherman yarn | Aran yarn |
| gauge | tension |
| ribbing | rib |
| seed stitch | moss stitch |
| sport yarn | DK yarn |
| stockinette stitch | stocking stitch |
| worsted yarn | Aran yarn |
| yarn wrapper | ball band |

## weights & lengths

$oz = g \times 0.0352$

$g = oz \times 28.35$

$in = cm \times 0.3937$

$cm = in \times 2.54$

$yd = m \times 0.9144$

$m = yd \times 1.0936$

## needle sizes

| US | metric | old UK & Canadian |
|---|---|---|
| 50 | 25 | – |
| 35 | 19 | – |
| 19 | 15 | – |
| 15 | 10 | 000 |
| 13 | 9 | 00 |
| 11 | 8 | 0 |
| 11 | 7.5 | 1 |
| 10½ | 7 | 2 |
| 10½ | 6.5 | 3 |
| 10 | 6 | 4 |
| 9 | 5.5 | 5 |
| 8 | 5 | 6 |
| 7 | 4.5 | 7 |
| 6 | 4 | 8 |
| 5 | 3.75 | 9 |
| 4 | 3.5 | – |
| 3 | 3.25 | 10 |
| 2 or 3 | 3 | 11 |
| 2 | 2.75 | 12 |
| 1 | 2.25 | 13 |
| 0 | 2 | 14 |

# keeping yarn stash notes

Once you have knitted your first project you will begin to acquire your first yarn stash. Initially, this will just be the yarn left over from your project that you save, just in case.

However, saved project yarn is just the start of your stash: soon you will be buying "must have" balls of yarn, whether you have any idea what you will do with them or not. Ask any long-time knitter about their yarn stash and they will invariably look both guilty and happy at the same time.

Keeping a yarn stash is fine, in fact it's great. It means you always have something to knit with and, if you are feeling a bit down, a quick rummage through your stash will instantly improve your mood. However, for your stash to be in any way useful, you do need to know what's in it. So be good and faithfully use the following pages to keep notes on all the yarns you buy.

Use a pencil to write your notes, then as you raid your stash and knit up yarns, you can rub them out, leaving space for all those

gorgeous new yarns you will certainly be buying. Make the yarn description as clear as you can, so that if a yarn in the stash becomes separated from its ball band you have a good chance of identifying what it is. You can even tape a sample of the yarn to the page if you want to.

Another very good idea is to keep a note of the project (if there is one) that you thought you might use the yarn for. That way, when it comes to your best friend's birthday, you can look in your notes and see if months ago you bought a beautiful yarn to make her a scarf—a yarn that you have now forgotten completely. Then you can just go to your stash and easily pick it out.

The first notes box opposite has been filled in to give you an idea of how best to record your own stash.

# my yarn stash

**yarn name:** Alpaca Choice Worsted

**yarn color and reference number:** Pale pink 274, 50g

**how many balls:** Four

**where bought:** Sarah's Stash Store

**notes:** Worsted weight yarn, very pale pink, slightly furry, loose twist, very soft. Use this to make a scarf, hat and mittens set for Luise; her birthday is 12 September.

**yarn name:**

**yarn color and reference number:**

**how many balls:**

**where bought:**

**notes:**

**yarn name:**

**yarn color and reference number:**

**how many balls:**

**where bought:**

**notes:**

**yarn name:**

**yarn color and reference number:**

**how many balls:**

**where bought:**

**notes:**

**yarn name:**

**yarn color and reference number:**

**how many balls:**

**where bought:**

**notes:**

**yarn name:**

**yarn color and reference number:**

**how many balls:**

**where bought:**

**notes:**

yarn name:

yarn color and reference number:

how many balls:

where bought:

notes:

---

yarn name:

yarn color and reference number:

how many balls:

where bought:

notes:

---

yarn name:

yarn color and reference number:

how many balls:

where bought:

notes:

---

yarn name:

yarn color and reference number:

how many balls:

where bought:

notes:

---

yarn name:

yarn color and reference number:

how many balls:

where bought:

notes:

---

yarn name:

yarn color and reference number:

how many balls:

where bought:

notes:

---

yarn name:

yarn color and reference number:

how many balls:

where bought:

notes:

---

yarn name:

yarn color and reference number:

how many balls:

where bought:

notes:

yarn name:

yarn color and reference number:

how many balls:

where bought:

notes:


yarn name:

yarn color and reference number:

how many balls:

where bought:

notes:


yarn name:

yarn color and reference number:

how many balls:

where bought:

notes:


yarn name:

yarn color and reference number:

how many balls:

where bought:

notes:


yarn name:

yarn color and reference number:

how many balls:

where bought:

notes:


yarn name:

yarn color and reference number:

how many balls:

where bought:

notes:


yarn name:

yarn color and reference number:

how many balls:

where bought:

notes:


yarn name:

yarn color and reference number:

how many balls:

where bought:

notes:

yarn name:

yarn color and reference number:

how many balls:

where bought:

notes:


yarn name:

yarn color and reference number:

how many balls:

where bought:

notes:


yarn name:

yarn color and reference number:

how many balls:

where bought:

notes:


yarn name:

yarn color and reference number:

how many balls:

where bought:

notes:


yarn name:

yarn color and reference number:

how many balls:

where bought:

notes:


yarn name:

yarn color and reference number:

how many balls:

where bought:

notes:


yarn name:

yarn color and reference number:

how many balls:

where bought:

notes:


yarn name:

yarn color and reference number:

how many balls:

where bought:

notes:

yarn name:

yarn color and reference number:

how many balls:

where bought:

notes:


yarn name:

yarn color and reference number:

how many balls:

where bought:

notes:


yarn name:

yarn color and reference number:

how many balls:

where bought:

notes:


yarn name:

yarn color and reference number:

how many balls:

where bought:

notes:


yarn name:

yarn color and reference number:

how many balls:

where bought:

notes:


yarn name:

yarn color and reference number:

how many balls:

where bought:

notes:


yarn name:

yarn color and reference number:

how many balls:

where bought:

notes:


yarn name:

yarn color and reference number:

how many balls:

where bought:

notes:

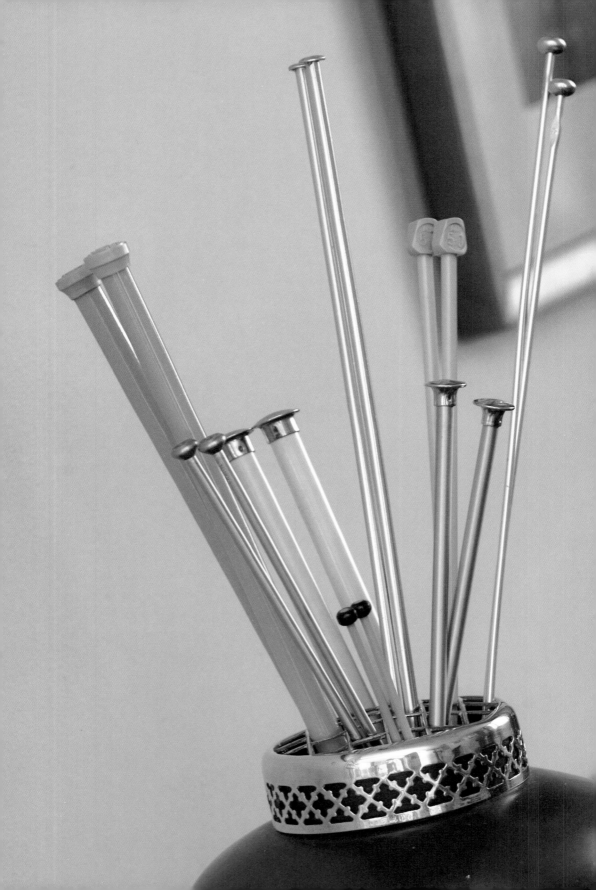

# knitting techniques

Knitting only has four fundamental techniques: cast on, knit, purl, and bind/cast off. Everything else is a variation of these basics, so once you have learnt them, all you need is practice.

## holding yarn and needles

There are two commonly used ways of holding the yarn and needles for knitting, so try them both and use whichever feels most comfortable.

In the USA and UK the usual way is to hold the left-hand needle rather like a knife and the right-hand needle rather like a pen. The working yarn goes over the index finger, under the second finger, and over the ring finger of the right hand: this helps control the stitch tension. The right index finger moves back and forth to wind the yarn around the right-hand needle.

The other method, often known as "the continental method," also holds the right-hand needle like a pen, but the left-hand needle is held between the thumb and second finger. The yarn goes over the left index finger, under the second and ring fingers, and over the little finger. The left index finger is held aloft and moves back and forth to wind the yarn around the right-hand needle.

## slip knot

The starting point for all knitting is a slip knot. There are a couple of ways of making this, but the end result is the same.

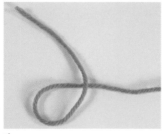

1 Form a loop by laying the tail end of the yarn over the ball end.

2 Bring the tail end under the loop. Slip the tip of a knitting needle under this tail end, as shown.

3 Pull on both ends of the yarn and the slip knot will tighten around the needle. After you have knitted the first couple of rows, you can pull gently on the tail end of the yarn to tighten the first stitch, if need be.

# thumb cast on

This cast on gives an elastic edge that matches in well with garter, rib, and seed/moss stitch. As you become familiar with this cast on you will get better at judging how far from the end of the yarn you need to make the slip knot in order to cast on the required number of stitches for a project.

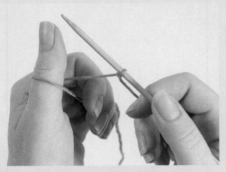

1 Make a slip knot about 20in/50cm from the end of the yarn. This knot will be the first stitch. Hold the needle with the knot in your right hand. *From front to back, wind the tail end of the yarn around your left thumb.

2 Put the tip of the needle under the loop of yarn around your thumb.

3 With your right index finger, lift the ball end of the yarn over the tip of the needle. Drop the yarn off your finger.

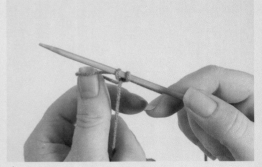

4 Pull the ball end of the yarn through the loop around your thumb, slipping the loop off your thumb as you do so. Pull gently on the tail end of the yarn to tighten the stitch.

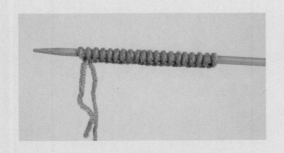

5 Repeat from * until you have cast the required number of stitches onto the needle.

# cable cast on

This method of casting on produces a firm edge that matches in perfectly with stockinette/stocking stitch.

1 Make a slip knot 6in/15cm from the end of the yarn. This knot will be the first stitch. Hold the needle with the knot in your left hand. From left to right, insert the tip of the right-hand needle into the front of the knot. *Wind the ball end of the yarn around the tip of the right-hand needle.

2 Pull the loop of yarn around the tip of the right-hand needle through the slip knot.

3 Slip the loop of yarn on the right-hand needle onto the left-hand needle and pull gently on the ball end of the yarn to tighten the stitch.

4 For all subsequent stitches, insert the right-hand needle between the two previous stitches, instead of through the stitch.

5 Repeat from * until you have cast the required number of stitches onto the needle.

# knit stitch

This is the first and most basic stitch you need to learn to start knitting.
First, cast on the required number of stitches.

1 Hold the needle with the stitches in your left hand. *From left to right, insert the tip of the right-hand needle into the front of the first stitch.

2 Wind the working yarn around the tip of the right-hand needle, going under and then over the needle.

3 Pull the loop of yarn on the tip of the right-hand needle through the stitch on the left-hand needle.

4 Keeping the new stitch on the right-hand needle, slip the first stitch off the left-hand needle. You have knitted one stitch. Repeat from * until you have knitted all the stitches on the left-hand needle. Then swap the needles in your hands and you are ready to begin again.

# purl stitch

This is the other basic stitch used in knitting. Once you have learned this, you can work any stitch pattern.

1 Hold the needle with the stitches in your left hand. *From right to left, insert the tip of the right-hand needle into the front of the first stitch.

2 From front to back, wind the working yarn over the tip of the right-hand needle.

3 Pull the loop on the tip of the right-hand needle through the stitch on the left-hand needle.

4 Keeping the new stitch on the right-hand needle, slip the first stitch off the left-hand needle. You have purled one stitch. Repeat from * until you have purled all the stitches on the left-hand needle. Then swap the needles in your hands and you are ready to begin again.

# binding/casting off

This is the way you finish off your knitting, securing the stitches so that they don't unravel. It is shown here on a knit row, but can be worked equally well on a purl row: just purl the stitches instead of knitting them.

1 Knit the first two stitches in the row.

2 *Use the tip of the left-hand needle to lift the first stitch over the second one. Drop this stitch off both needles.

3 Knit another stitch and repeat from *, casting off all the stitches in turn.

4 When you have just one stitch left on the right-hand needle, pull gently to open it up a little and slip it off the needle. Cut the yarn 6in/15cm from the knitting, slip the cut end through the last stitch and pull gently on the cut end to tighten the stitch.

# knitted fabrics

Knit and purl stitches form the foundation for all knitted fabrics. Here are swatches of the four most popular knits.

*garter stitch* This is the most basic knitted fabric as it is made up entirely of knit stitches.

To work garter stitch cast on as many stitches as you require.

Knit every row. It really is that simple.

*rib stitch* This is usually used to make cuffs and collars as it opens out and springs back easily.

To work rib stitch cast on an odd number of stitches.

Row 1: [K1, p1] rep to last st, k1.

Row 2: [P1, k1] rep to last st, p1.

Rep rows 1–2 until you have worked the required number of rib rows.

*stockinette/stocking stitch (st st)* The most popular of all knitted fabrics, this is worked with alternate rows of knit and purl stitches. The other side of this fabric is called reverse stockinette/stocking stitch (rev st st).

To work stockinette/stocking stitch, cast on as many stitches as you require.

Knit the first row.

Purl the second row.

Rep this process, knitting and purling the alternate rows.

*seed/moss stitch* This is a decorative stitch that makes a flat, firm border on garments and accessories.

To work seed/moss stitch cast on an odd number of stitches.

Row 1: [K1, p1] rep to last st, k1.

Rep row 1 until you have worked the required number of seed/moss rows.

# increases

Increasing is the process of adding more stitches to a row to shape the knitting. There are various different ways of doing this; shown here are the two methods used in the projects in this book (see pages 56–67).

*increase (inc)* This method involves knitting twice into a stitch.

1 Knit to the position of the increase. Knit into the next stitch in the usual way (see page 32). However, do not drop the original stitch off the left-hand needle.

2 Now knit into the back of the same original stitch and then drop it off the left-hand needle.

You have made two stitches out of one and so increased by one stitch.

*make one (M1)* This method involves creating a new stitch between two existing ones and is almost completely invisible.

1 Knit to the position of the increase. Using the tip of the left-hand needle, pick up the loop between the next two stitches. Pick it up by putting the tip of the needle through the front of the loop.

2 Knit into the back of the picked-up loop on the left-hand needle.

You have created a completely new stitch and so increased by one stitch.

# decreases

Decreasing is the process of taking away stitches in a row to shape the knitting. Again, there are various different ways of doing this, but shown here are the two methods used in the projects in this book. These decreases slant in different directions, so when used at either end of a row, they mirror each other effectively.

*knit two together (k2tog)*  This method involves knitting two stitches together to make one. This decrease slants to the right on a knit row.

1 Knit to the position of the decrease. From left to right, put the tip of the right-hand needle through the front of the second stitch from the end of the left-hand needle, then through the first one. Knit the two stitches together as if they were one.

You have made two stitches into one and so decreased by one stitch.

*slip, slip, knit two together (ssk)*  This method involves slipping stitches and then knitting them together. This decrease slants to the left on a knit row.

1 Knit to the position of the decrease. Insert the right-hand needle into the next stitch and slip it from the left-hand to the right-hand needle, without knitting it.

2 Repeat Step 1 to slip a second stitch from the left-hand to the right-hand needle, again without knitting it.

3 Put the tip of the left-hand needle through the two slipped stitches, putting it through in front of the right-hand needle, as shown. Knit the two slipped stitches together as if they were one.

You have made two stitches into one and so decreased by one stitch.

# bobbles

These are a simple and fun way to add texture to a piece of plain knitting. They are also used with cables (see page 39) to produce traditional Aran designs.

1 Knit to the position of the bobble. Using the same method as for inc (see page 36), knit into the front and back of the stitch, but do this twice before dropping the original stitch. You have made four stitches from one.

2 Turn the work around—swapping the needles in your hands—and purl these four stitches. Turn the work again and knit the four stitches. Turn the work yet again and purl the four stitches again, as shown.

3 Turn the work for the last time. Make the first two stitches into one using ssk (see page 37). Then turn the next two stitches into one using k2tog, as shown (also see page 37).

4 Using the same method as for binding/casting off (see page 34), lift the first stitch over the second one to end up with just one stitch. Knit to the end of the row, or the next bobble, whichever comes first.

Right: these three bobbles have three rows of plain stockinette/stocking stitch worked between each one.

# cables

Cabling is one of those techniques that looks difficult, but is in fact very simple. All you are doing is swapping the positions on the needle of groups of stitches. Shown here is cable six, but you can cable two, four, or eight stitches just as easily. Larger numbers are perfectly possible, but can be trickier to cable neatly. For maximum effect, cables are usually worked in stockinette/stocking stitch on a background of reverse stockinette/stocking stitch, as shown here. However, they also look beautiful worked on a background of seed/moss stitch (see page 60).

### *cable six front (C6F)* A front cable twists to the left.

1 Purl to the position of the cable. Take the yarn to the back. Slip the next three stitches on the left-hand needle onto a cable needle and leave it at the front of the work.

2 Knit the next three stitches that are on the left-hand needle.

3 Now knit the three stitches on the cable needle. Purl to the end of the row.

### *cable six back (C6B)*
A back cable twists to the right.

1 Work a back cable in the same way as a front cable, but once you have slipped the three stitches onto the cable needle, leave it at the back of the work instead of at the front while you knit the next three stitches on the left-hand needle. Then knit the stitches on the cable needle.

Right: this swatch of C6F is worked over eight rows; that is to say, the cable is twisted on every eighth row.

# swiss darning

Also known as "duplicate stitch" this is a way of working different-colored stitches onto a piece of knitting once it is finished. Always work Swiss darning using a yarn that is the same weight as the yarn the fabric is knitted in or it won't look very neat.

*a vertical row* Use this method to work vertical rows of colored stitches.

1 Thread a knitter's sewing needle with a long length of yarn. From the back, bring the needle up through the knitted fabric at the base of a stitch. *Take the needle under the two loops of the stitch above, as shown.

2 Gently pull the yarn through. Then take the needle back down through the base of the stitch, where it came out.

3 Bring the yarn up through the knitted fabric at the base of the next stitch up in the column. Repeat from * until the row is stitched.

*a horizontal row*
Use this method to work horizontal rows of stitches.

1 From the back, bring the needle up through the knitted fabric at the base of a stitch. Take the needle under the two loops of the stitch above and back down where it came out, as before. Bring the needle up through the base of the next stitch to the left to work the horizontal row.

Above: Swiss darning is the best technique for working fine, outline motifs, such as this little heart.

# bead and sequin knitting

This is another technique that looks complicated, but is in fact easy to work. Beads and sequins will add instant glamor and sparkle to the plainest piece of knitting.

**bead knitting** Choose beads with a hole large enough to fit over your yarn when it is doubled.

1 Before you start the piece of knitting, you must thread all the beads you are going to need onto the yarn. To do this, thread a beading needle with a short length of beading thread, knot the ends together and trim any excess thread close to the knot. Slip the end of the yarn through the loop of thread. Then just slip the beads onto the needle, down the thread, and so onto the knitting yarn.

2 On a knit row, knit to the position of the first bead. Bring the yarn forward between the needles and slide a bead up to the work.

4 Leaving the bead at the front of the work, sitting in front of the slipped stitch, take the yarn to the back. Knit to the end of the row, or the next bead, knitting the stitch after the bead as firmly as you can.

3 Slip the next stitch purlwise, slipping it from the left-hand needle onto the right-hand needle, without knitting it.

**sequin knitting** Sequins have only a small hole in the middle, so they are best used on a fairly lightweight yarn.

1 Use the same method for knitting in beads to knit sequins into your work. Bring the yarn forward, slide the sequin down, slip the next stitch purlwise, then take the yarn back.

Left: this method of knitting in beads and sequins can only be worked on every other stitch and every other row. Sequins knitted in in this way will overlap one another (depending on how large they are), and can cover up the knitted fabric completely.

# joining in new yarn

When you reach the end of a ball of yarn you need to join in a new one in order to continue knitting your project. You also use this method to join in a different-colored yarn if you are knitting stripes.

**1** It is always best to join in new yarn at the end of a row. To knit one row, the remaining yarn must measure approximately four times the width of the knitting.

Tie the new yarn in a loose single knot around the end of the old yarn. Slide the knot up to the work and pull it tight. Leave at least a 6in/15cm tail on each piece of yarn.

# weaving in ends

When you have finished your knitting, you need to weave in any ends from casting on, binding/casting off, and joining in new yarn.

**1** Thread a knitter's sewing needle with the tail of yarn. Take the needle back and forth, not up and over, through the backs of the stitches. Go through approximately four stitches in one direction, then work back through the last two again. Cut the end of the yarn short.

# blocking

Once you have finished your knitting project, it will benefit from being blocked. This process smoothes out the fabric, helps hide any small imperfections in tension, and makes the project much easier to sew up. And it really doesn't take very long to do.

**1** On a blocking board (see page 51) or an ironing board, lay out your project pieces, without stretching them. Measure each piece and gently ease them to the correct size. Pin the pieces to the board by pushing dressmaker's pins through the edge stitches into the board.

Carefully following the instructions on the yarn ball band, press all the pieces. Leave them pinned out until they are completely cold.

Take out the pins and you are ready to sew up your project.

# sewing up

This is the last stage of making your project, and doing it well can give your project a really professional look. Take your time and your seams will be smooth and neat.

**1** Thread a knitter's sewing needle with a long length of the yarn you used to knit the project in. (If the yarn is very fine or breaks easily, use a stronger one in the same fiber and color.) Here, a contrast color yarn has been used so you can clearly see what is happening. Secure the yarn on the back of one piece of the project by taking it over a couple of stitches, a couple of times.

**2** Bring the needle to the front of the fabric, bringing it up between the first two stitches on the first row.

**3** Right-side up, lay the project piece to be joined next to the first piece. From the front, take the needle through the fabric between the first two stitches on the first row, and up under the bars of two stitches.

**4** Pull the yarn through. Take the needle back through where it came out on the first project piece, and up under the bars of two stitches. Continue in this way, zigzagging between the two pieces and taking the needle under two stitch bars each time. Gently pull up the stitches to close the seam as you work.

Left: worked neatly a mattress stitched seam blends in well with the knitted fabric.

# knitting tips

Ask a long-time knitter to demonstrate a technique you've read in a book, but struggled to understand, and she'll usually add in some little tip that makes it easier to grasp. So here are 35 of those little tips, just to make your knitting life that bit simpler.

### 1. From the middle

Use the end of yarn in the middle of the ball, not the (admittedly, easier to find) end on the outside. You might have to fish around in the ball to find the end, but when you pull on it to release more yarn, the ball won't roll off your lap, across the floor, and under the table.

### 2. Sew smart

Leave very long tails of yarn when you cast on and bind/cast off and use these tails to sew up the seams of your project. Some knitting books tell you not to do this, but if you are a reasonably good sewer-up, and so less likely to have to unpick, then this is a perfectly valid way to sew seams. It also means that you get a neater finish with fewer annoying ends to weave in.

### 3. Cable masterclass

When you start or end a cable on a cast on or bound/cast off row, the cable section of the knitted fabric tends to flare out a little. There is an easy way to correct this and keep the cast on and bound/cast off edges neat and smooth. Cast on the required number of stitches, minus half the number for each cable section. For example if you have to cast on 28 stitches, which includes three cable sections of six stitches each, 18 cable stitches in total, you would in fact cast on 9 stitches for the cable sections plus the remaining 10, making 19 stitches cast on. Knit the first row and work one increase into each stitch in each cable section, bringing each section up to the required six stitches. When you come to bind/cast off the work, on the last row work k2tog across the six stitches of the cable section, bringing each one down to three stitches, then cast off in the usual way.

### 4. Which cast on to use?

The thumb cast on (see page 30) is good with garter stitch (above left), rib, and seed/moss stitch; the ridged edge blends in well with all these stitch patterns. The cable cast on (see page 31) works well with stockinette/stocking stitch (above, right), as the slanting stitches it produces complement the stitch pattern.

## 5. Twisted stitches

If you've dropped some stitches and successfully picked them up, how do you then tell if they are the right way around on the needle? It's easy: a stitch laid out flat is a loop of yarn and the right-hand leg of that loop must always be on the front of the knitting needle as it faces you. This applies to stitches on both knit and purl rows.

## 6. Picking up dropped stitches to make knit and purl stitches

On stockinette/stocking stitch, work from the front to pick up every stitch. On garter stitch, and knit and purl stitch patterns, work with the right or wrong side facing you, depending on whether, on the right side of the work, you want the stitch to lie smooth (a knit stitch, so right-side facing), or form a bump (a purl stitch, so wrong-side facing).

## 7. Color knitting tangles: method 1

If you are working an intarsia or Fair Isle pattern, then you can wind your yarns onto bobbins to prevent them tangling. However, if you don't have bobbins then you can use the shoebox trick. Punch as many holes in the lid of a shoe box as you have colors of yarn. Make the holes about 1/2in/1cm across. Put the balls of yarn in the box, feed an end through each hole and tape the lid down. The yarns will twist around themselves as you turn the work, but they won't tangle, and it's easy enough to untwist them, just turn the work the other way.

## 8. Saving for the future

Don't just put all the leftover yarn from a project into your stash. Put at least some of it into a re-sealable plastic bag with a note of which project it came from and store it safely. That way, if in the future you damage the garment you can darn it, repair a seam, or even replace a collar or cuff using perfectly matching yarn.

## 9. Beading buttons

Add a finishing touch to a project by beading the buttons. Bring the needle up through the hole in the button, thread on two or more beads, then take the needle down through the other hole. Go through the button and beads a few more times to attach them firmly. If the holes in the beads are tiny, then use a beading needle and thread to sew on the buttons and beads.

## 10. Neat and tidy

If you are knitting a garter stitch or stockinette/stocking stitch project where the edges will show—for example, a scarf—then work a simple selvedge along the row edges to make them look especially neat. For garter stitch, slip the first stitch on every row you knit. If you are working the project in stockinette/stocking stitch, slip the first stitch on every knit row only. Both these methods will produce a chain-effect selvedge that will look tidier than plain row ends.

### 11. Zippers

These come in quite a limited color range and it is unlikely that you will find one that is a perfect match for your yarn. In this case, choose a zipper that is darker rather than lighter in color than the yarn; it will show less.

### 12. Left handers

Many left-handed people knit in the right-handed fashion, especially if they were taught by a right-hander. However, if you do knit left-handed it can be difficult to follow techniques in a book, which are invariably shown being worked right-handed. A simple trick is to hold the diagram up to a mirror and look at it in reverse. Better still, get a friend to hold it up so that you can copy it while looking in the mirror.

### 13. All wound up

If you don't have a ball winder, this is the way to wind up a skein of yarn so that you can pull the yarn from the center. 1 Leaving a tail of yarn hanging over your hand, wind the yarn in a figure eight around your thumb and index finger. Wind about 1 yard/meter in this way. 2 Fold the figure eight in half, sliding it off your finger and thumb. 3 Being careful not to trap the tail of yarn you left in Step 1, start to wind the yarn around the folded bundle to make your ball. Wind loosely at first so the center of the ball isn't too firm or it can be difficult to pull out the yarn initially.

### 14. Picking up stitches

It's surprising how many learn-to-knit books still explain how to pick up a dropped stitch with the tips of your knitting needles. If you have just dropped the stitch and it's only slipped down one row, then this isn't too hard to do. However, if it has slipped down several rows then you are going to struggle to get it back. Use a crochet hook instead, it's so much easier. Put the hook through the dropped stitch, catch the first strand of the ladder of yarn and pull it through the stitch. Continue in this way until you have picked up all of the dropped stitches.

### 15. Reversing shaping

You will often come across the following in a knitting pattern:

**Left Front**
Work as for Right Front, reversing all shapings.

What this means is that if you decreased at the end of a row for the Right Front, you must decrease at the beginning of the same row for the Left Front. In this way you will produce two pieces that are mirror images of one another. If you are at all confused as to what you should be doing on each row, write out the Right Front pattern, reversing all the shaping instructions, to make a pattern for the Left Front. Much quicker than getting it wrong and having to start again.

**16. Make and match** You can make buttons to perfectly match your yarn by using the self-cover buttons that dressmakers use. Buy a button kit of the right size and knit a small square, wide and deep enough to cover the template on the back of the button kit. To make the knitted fabric dense enough to stop the button showing through, you may need to go down one or two needle sizes. Use the square to cover the button, following the manufacturer's instructions. If the fabric is too bulky to tuck into the button, either stitch a circle using a sewing machine and a small straight stitch, then cut off the excess knitting, or knit a circle instead of a square.

If your yarn is too chunky to knit a button cover in, try splitting the plies and knitting the square with just half of them.

**17. Fixing baggy stitches** Before blocking a finished piece of knitting, spread it out flat and examine it carefully. If there is an occasional baggy stitch, you can use a knitter's pin (see page 13) to fix it. Slip the pin under the first loop of the stitch next to the baggy one and gently tweak the stitch to tighten the baggy one a little. Repeat this on the next one or two stitches along until the excess yarn from the baggy stitch has been incorporated evenly into the knitting.

**19. Loose last stitch: method 1** The last stitch of a cast off has an irritating habit of being baggy and spoiling your smooth edge. To fix this, before you knit the last stitch on the cast off row, use the tip of the right-hand needle to pick up the top of the stitch immediately below, on the back of the work. Slip this loop onto the tip of the left-hand needle and knit it and the last stitch together. This will tighten the last cast off stitch.

**18. Charting your way** By the time a knitting chart has been scaled down to fit onto the page of a book or magazine, it can be so small that each square is tiny, making it really hard to follow. Don't struggle and strain your eyes, enlarge the pattern to the biggest possible size on a photocopier. If it is a color-work chart, then, obviously, a color photocopy is best. If you have to copy the chart in black and white, spend a little time coloring over the squares with colored pencils. It can also be helpful to color a black and white symbol chart: colored squares can be easier to see than symbols. This also applies to stitch pattern charts, which are usually given as symbols only. Coloring all the purl squares pink and all the knit ones green can save you making errors.

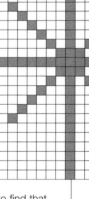

**20. Using graph paper** Have you ever designed a knitting motif on graph paper, very carefully plotting out one stitch per square, then knitted it up only to find that the finished knitted motif is distorted? This is because a stitch isn't square, it is in fact wider than it is high. To successfully draw a motif onto graph paper and have it knit up correctly, you need to use knitter's ratio graph paper, which you will find at the back of this journal. Design your motifs on this with confidence.

## 21. Perfect buttonhole

Use this trick to cure that ugly loose stitch you get on one side of a two-row buttonhole. When you are casting on the stitches to work back across the buttonhole, cast on using the cable method. With the last cast on stitch still on the right-hand needle, bring the yarn forward between the needles. Slip the last stitch onto the left-hand needle. Pull gently on the yarn to tighten the stitch, then take the yarn back again. Work the rest of the row.

## 22. Fixing baggy intarsia

Many people find that when working intarsia knitting, no matter how carefully they twist the yarns at the back of the fabric, the edge stitches of an intarsia motif, particularly on the purl rows, are a bit baggy. There are a couple of ways to fix this. You can use a knitter's pin to ease out the baggy stitches (see page 48). Alternatively, when you weave in the ends of the yarns (see page 42), carefully weave them through the backs of the stitches either side of the color join. You need to ensure that the wrong color yarns do not show through on the front of the knitting, but done well this technique can tighten up the baggy stitches beautifully.

## 23. A fine finish

If you are working rib or seed/moss stitch, then cast off in pattern for the neatest edge. Knit the knit stitches and cast them off in the usual way. Purl the purl stitches, then take the yarn to the back of the work before lifting the previous stitch over the purled one.

## 24. Picking up stitches evenly

Sometimes a pattern instruction will read:

Pick up 40 stitches evenly around the neckline.

The cumulative number of stitches in the front and back panels (joined at the shoulders to make the neck opening), may be more than 40, and the decreases only confuse matters further, so you can't pick up stitch-for-stitch. The best way to achieve an even pick-up is to divide the neckline into halves and then quarters, marking each division with a knitter's pin. You can do the dividing by eye, or if you prefer, use a tape measure. Now you just need to pick up ten stitches across each quarter and you will have picked up evenly right around the neckline. For larger numbers of stitches, just sub-divide the neckline further.

## 25. Joining in

It is always best to join in new yarn at the end of a row. To establish whether or not you have enough yarn to knit one more row, lay it out as shown.

You must have a length of yarn approximately four times the width of the knitting to knit a single row.

### 26. Moth alert!

Clothes moths are the arch enemy of all knitters and once they get into your yarn stash, they are very hard to get rid of. The damage they cause is both heartbreaking and alarmingly rapid. Use mothballs or other anti-moth products to protect both your woolen clothes and your stash at all times. If you separate you stash into different types of yarn, remember that you need to protect all yarns made from animal fibers (so silk and mixed fiber yarns as well as pure wool), as these are what moths like best.

### 27. Beading on fancy yarns

The best general advice is, don't do this. The beads tend to get lost in the yarn and sliding them down its length can spoil a textured yarn. If you feel you must bead a fancy yarn, knit a swatch to see what it looks like, then carefully unravel it and look at the yarn to see if the beads damaged it in any way.

### 28. Loose last stitch: method 2

There is another way of fixing the loose last stitch of a cast off. Slip the first stitch on the previous row of knitting. This will make the last stitch of the cast off tighter, but does leave a slipped stitch to look out for when sewing up the project.

### 29. Safe unraveling

If the worst comes to the worst and you do have to unravel a few (or a lot of) rows of knitting, you can make sure you don't go to far by running a strand of contrast yarn or thread through the row you want to unravel down to. Thread a knitter's sewing needle (see page 13) with the contrast yarn and take it through the right-hand loop of each stitch across the row. Unravel the knitting and when you get to the marked row the contrast yarn will act like a flexible knitting needle and hold the stitches. Then just pick them up with an actual knitting needle, following the path of the yarn to ensure that each stitch is the right way around.

### 30. Binding/casting off on knit and purl rows

If you bind/cast off on a knit row, the cast off will lie across the front of the work. If you bind/cast off on a purl row the stitches lie flatter across the end of the work, which can look tidier on an end that isn't going to be sewn in; for example, the end of a scarf.

### 31. Making a blocking board

Buy a piece of MDF approximately 1yd/1m by 33in/50cm (or as large as you can easily store somewhere dry). Cover one side of this with three layers of woolen quilter's batting/wadding, folding the batting over the edges and stapling it in place on the back. Keep the corners as neat as possible. Cover the batting/wadding with a piece of gingham fabric, folding it over the edges and stapling as before. Take your time over this, making sure that the gingham pattern is as square as possible to the edges of the board.

When you are pinning out your project pieces, use the gingham pattern to keep straight lines straight and to square up corners neatly. Push the pins through the edge stitches of the knitting at an angle, so that they slide into the layers of batting/wadding.

### 32. Dropped stitch emergency

Keep a couple of small safety pins pinned to the inside top of your knitting bag. If you drop a stitch halfway across a row, put a safety pin through it to stop it dropping down further while you find your crochet hook to pick up the stitch (see page 47). This way you prevent the stitch dropping even further down the knitting before you can pick it up.

### 33. Highlighting patterns

If a pattern gives more than one size for a garment, take the time to go through it first and highlight all the bits that are relevant to the size you are knitting. It's very easy to get distracted and knit the wrong number of stitches on a row, and before you know it you are in a complete muddle. It's a good idea to photocopy the pattern and highlight the copy, leaving the pattern book unmarked for the next time you want to knit the same project, but in a different size.

### 34. Color knitting tangles: method 2

If you find the shoe box (see page 46) a bit restrictive, another way to control your yarns in color knitting is to thread each one through a drinking straw before you start work. Again, they will twist around one another, but they are far less likely to tangle.

### 35. Swiss darning on intarsia

If an intarsia pattern calls for a single stitch line as part of the motif, then ignore it while you are knitting the project. Once the piece is finished, add in the line using duplicate stitch. This is much easier and tidier than trying to work the line in intarsia.

# my tips

Use these pages to make a note of any other useful knitting tips
and tricks you may learn.

tip:

notes:

tip:

notes:

tip:

notes:

tip:

notes:

tip:

notes:

tip:

notes:

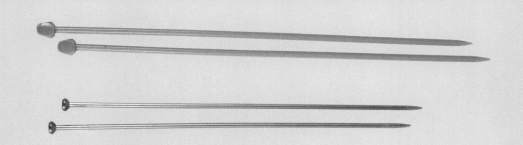

tip:

notes:

tip:

notes:

tip:

notes:

tip:

notes:

tip:

notes:

tip:

notes:

tip:

notes:

tip:

notes:

tip:

notes:

tip:

notes:

tip:

notes:

tip:

notes:

tip:

notes:

tip:

notes:

tip:

notes:

tip:

notes:

tip:

notes:

tip:

notes:

tip:

notes:

tip:

notes:

tip:

notes:

tip:

notes:

# star cravat scarf

Snug, stylish, and simple to wear, this little scarf will be a staple item in your wardrobe. It's easy to knit and the embroidery is simple to work, but the garter stitch borders, rib sections, and shaped end make it a step above the usual plain strip-of-knitting scarf.

The project uses three stitch patterns—all easy ones—and just very basic shaping techniques. The embroidered star is charted for you, all you have to do is stitch it!

## you will need

Two 1³/₄oz/50g balls of RY Silk Wool DK in Porcelain (A)

Small amount of RY Silk Wool DK in Lime Wash (B) for the embroidery

Pair of US 6/4mm knitting needles

Pair of US 5/3.75mm knitting needles

Knitter's sewing needle

## tension

24 stitches and 28 rows to 4in/10cm over stockinette/stocking stitch using RY Silk Wool DK and US 6/4mm needles.

## abbreviations

See page 20.

SCARF

Using the thumb method, US 6/4mm needles and A, cast on 31 sts.

**Row 1 (WS):** Sl1, k to end.

This row establishes garter stitch with selvedge edge.

Work seven more rows in garter stitch with selvedge edge.

**Row 9:** Sl1, k4, p20, k5.

**Row 10:** Sl1, k to end.

Rows 9–10 establish 2-row stitch patt.

Rep 2-row stitch patt until the

work measures 6¾in/17cm from cast-on edge, ending with a row 9.

Change to US 5/3.75mm needles.

**Next row:** [K1, p1] rep to last st, k1.

**Next row:** [P1, k1] rep to last st, p1.

These last two rows establish rib.

Work nine more rows in rib.

Change to US 6/4mm needles.

**Next row:** [P2, p2tog] rep twice more, p7, [p2tog, p2] rep

twice more. *(25 sts)*

**Next row:** Sl1, k to end.

**Next row:** Sl1, p to end.

These last two rows establish st st with selvedge edge. Work in st st with selvedge edge until the work measures 21in/53cm from end of ribbed section (or until it is long enough to sit comfortably around your neck), ending with a purl row.

Change to US 5/3.75mm needles.

**Next row:** [K1, p1] rep to last st, k1.

**Next row:** [P1, k1] rep to last st, p1.

These last two rows establish rib.

Work four more rows in rib.

Change to US 6/4mm needles.

**Next row:** [K2, M1] rep twice more, k13, [M1, k2], rep twice more. *(31 sts)*

**Next row:** Sl1, p to end.

**Next row:** Sl1, k1, ssk, k to last 4 sts, k2tog, k2.

These last two rows establish 2-row stitch patt that decreases the number of sts by 2 with each repeat.

Rep 2-row patt eleven more times. *(7 sts)*

**Next row:** Purl.

Bind/cast off.

LOOP

Using the cable method, US 5/3.75mm needles and A, cast on 20 sts.

**Row 1:** Knit.

**Row 2:** Purl.

Rep rows 1–2 once more.

Bind/cast off.

EMBROIDERY

Using the knitter's sewing needle and B, and following the chart below, Swiss-darn the star onto the front of the scarf, placing it centrally and 5 rows up from the top of the garter stitch border.

FINISHING

Block st st sections of scarf and the loop. Sew the loop to the back of the first ribbed section of the scarf, sewing one end to the third column of knit stitches in on each side.

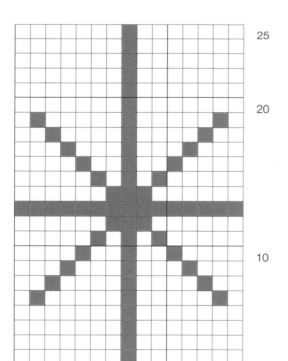

Above: tucking the shaped end of the scarf into the loop will keep it snugly in place around your neck.

# cream & caramel cushion

This project requires no shaping and is knitted all in one piece, so you can concentrate on working the textured stitches. The pattern makes use of different stitch textures, but it isn't difficult to follow. The cable repeat is simple, and using seed/moss stitch as the background will help eliminate the baggy stitches that tend to occur along the edges of cables.

## you will need

Two 1³/₄oz/50g balls of Debbie Bliss Pure Cotton in Taupe (A)

Two 1³/₄oz/50g balls of Debbie Bliss Stella in Cream (B)

Pair of US 7/4.5mm knitting needles

Cable needle

Three 1in/2.5cm diameter pearl buttons

18 x 14in/45 x 35cm cushion pad

## tension

19 stitches and 25 rows to 4in/10cm over stockinette/stocking stitch using Debbie Bliss Pure Cotton and US 7/4.5mm needles.

## abbreviations

**MB** = Knit 4 times into stitch, turn, p4, turn, k4, turn, p4, turn, ssk, k2tog, pass first stitch over second stitch.

See also page 20.

## CONTRAST BOBBLES

Cut five 28-in/70-cm lengths of B before you start the project, ready to knit the contrast bobbles with.

When working a contrast bobble, use one end of the contrast yarn to make the foundation stitch in the purl row below the bobble row, as instructed in the pattern. Use the technique for joining in new yarn and ensure that the shortest tail of yarn is 2in/5cm long. To work the next stitch in the main color, bring the main yarn across over the tails of contrast yarn. On the bobble row, work the bobbles into the foundation stitch as instructed, making sure you use the long tail of contrast yarn. When the bobble is complete, drop the end of the contrast yarn and ignore it until the knitting is complete. Then untie the knot joining in the contrast yarn and pull firmly on the tails to neaten the bobbles. Tie the ends in a secure double knot then weave them in.

## CUSHION COVER

Using the thumb method and A, cast on 65 sts.

**Row 1 (RS):** [P1, k1] to last st, p1.

**Row 2:** [K1, p1] to last st, k1.

These two rows establish rib.

Work five more rows in rib.

**Row 8 (buttonhole row 1):** Rib 16, bind/cast off 3 sts, rib next 11 sts, bind/cast off 3 sts, rib next 11 sts, bind/cast off 3 sts, rib next 15 sts.

**Row 9 (buttonhole row 2):** Rib 16, cast on 3 sts, rib 12, cast on 3 sts, rib 12, cast on 3 sts, rib 16.

Rib five more rows.

Change to B

Work one more row in rib.

**Row 16:** [K1, p1] to last st, k1.

**Row 17:** [K1, p1] to last st, k1.

These two rows establish seed/moss stitch.

Work five more rows in seed/moss stitch.

**Row 23:** Purl.

**Row 24:** Knit.

These two rows establish rev st st.

Work twenty-four more rows in rev st st.

**Row 49:** [K1, p1] to last st, k1.

**Row 50:** [K1, p1] to last st, k1.

These two rows establish seed/moss stitch.

Work five more rows in seed/moss stitch.

Change to A

**Row 56 (ridge row):** Knit.

**Row 57:** Knit.

**Row 58:** Purl.

These two rows establish st st.

Work five more rows in st st.

**Row 64 (bobble foundation row):** P10A, p1B, p10A, p1B, p10A, p1B, p10A, p1B, p10A, p1B, p10A.

**Row 65 (bobble row):** K10A, MB in B, k10A, MB in B, k10A, MB in B, k10A, MB in B, k10A, MB in B, k10A.

Work five rows st st.

**Row 71:** [K1, p1] to last st, k1.

**Row 72:** [K1, p1] to last st, k1.

These two rows establish seed/moss stitch.

Work 12 more rows in seed/moss stitch.

**Row 85:** Seed/moss 13, [k6, seed/moss 5] rep twice more, k6, seed/moss 13.

**Row 86:** Seed/moss 13, [p6, seed/moss 5] rep twice more, p6, seed/moss 13.

Rep rows 85–86 four more times.

**Row 95:** Seed/moss 13, C6F,

seed/moss 5, C6F, seed/moss 5, C6B, seed/moss 5, C6B, seed/moss 13.

**Row 96:** Seed/moss 13, [p6, seed/moss 5] rep twice more, p6, seed/moss 13.

**Row 97:** Seed/moss 13, [k6, seed/moss 5] rep twice more, k6, seed/moss 13.

Rep rows 96–97 four more times.

Rep row 96 once more.

**Row 107:** Seed/moss 13, C6F, seed/moss 5, C6F, seed/moss 5, C6B, seed/moss 5, C6B, seed/moss 13.

Rows 96–107 establish 12-row cable patt.

Rep 12-row cable patt four more times.

**Row 156:** Seed/moss 13, [p6, seed/moss 5] rep twice more, p6, seed/moss 13.

**Row 157:** Seed/moss 13, [k6, seed/moss 5] rep twice more, k6, seed/moss 13.

Rep rows 156–157 twice more.

Change to B

Rep rows 156–157 twice more.

Rep row 156 once more.

**Row 167:** Seed/moss 13, C6F, seed/moss 5, C6F, seed/moss 5, C6B, seed/moss 5, C6B, seed/moss 13.

Rep 12-row cable patt once more.

**Row 180:** Seed/moss 13, [p6, seed/moss 5] rep twice more, p6, seed/moss 13.

**Row 181:** Seed/moss 13, [k6, seed/moss 5] rep twice

more, k6, seed/moss 13.

Rep rows 180–181 four more times.

Change to A

**Row 190 (ridge row):** Knit.

**Row 191:** Knit.

**Row 192:** Purl.

These two rows establish st st.

Work 39 more rows in st st.

Change to B

Work 25 more rows in st st.

Bind/cast off.

FINISHING

Block the cushion cover, but press only the st st and rev st st sections.

Right-side down, lay the cushion cover flat. Fold the buttonhole end over at the ridge row. Starting at the ridge row and using mattress stitch, sew the side seams. Fold the other end over at the ridge row, tucking the bound/cast off edge under the ribbed edge. Starting at the ridge row and using mattress stitch, sew the side seams. When you reach the rib, turn the cushion cover inside out and slip stitch the edges of the final rows of st st to the inside seams.

Sew on buttons to align with the buttonholes.

# stripy beaded bag

You rarely see vertical stripes in hand knitting because they involve long straight-line intarsia joins, which are tricky to keep neat and smooth. However, this pretty bag gets its stripes by simply cheating—it is knitted in one piece from side-to-side, rather than top to bottom, so you are, in fact, just working horizontal stripes.
The pattern might look a bit complicated, but once you have done the simple shaping, it's actually only two rows repeated. The rest of the pattern information is telling you when to change colors and place beads.

## you will need

One 1¾oz/50g ball of Debbie Bliss Cashmerino Aran (A)

One 1¾oz/50g ball of Rowan Kid Classic (B)

One 1¾oz/50g ball of Louisa Harding Grace Silk & Wool (C)

Pair of US 4/3.5mm knitting needles

124 0.157in/4mm dark pink cube beads

Knitter's sewing needle

## tension

22 stitches and 32 rows to 4in/10cm over stockinette/stocking stitch using Debbie Bliss Cashmerino Aran and US 4/3.5mm needles.

Note: as this is a bag it is not necessary to achieve an exact tension.

## abbreviations

PB = place bead. Bring the yarn forward between the needles, slip the next stitch purlwise, slide a bead down the yarn to sit next to the needle, take the yarn back between the needles. Note: knit the next stitch firmly.

Note: thread all the beads onto A. You will use 104 of them in knitting the bag and the remaining 20 in knitting the handle.

BAG

Using the cable method and A, cast on 70 sts.

**Row 1 (WS):** Purl.

**Row 2 (RS):** K1, M1, k68, M1, k1. *(72 sts)*

**Row 3:** Purl.

Change to B

**Row 4:** K1, M1, k70, M1, k1. *(74 sts)*

**Row 5:** Purl.

**Row 6:** K1, M1, k72, M1, k1. *(76 sts)*

Change to C

**Row 7:** Purl.

**Row 8:** K1, M1, k74, M1, k1, cast on 14 sts. *(92 sts)*

**Row 9:** K7, p1, [k1, p1] three times, p78, cast on 14 sts. *(106 sts)*

**Row 10:** P7, k1, [p1, k1] three times, k78, [p1, k1] three times, k1, p7.

Change to A

**Row 11:** K7, p1, [k1, p1] three times, p78, [k1, p1]

three times, p1, k7.

**Row 12:** P7, k1, [p1, k1] three times, k78, [p1, k1] three times, k1, p7.

**Row 13:** K7, p1, [k1, p1] three times, p78, [k1, p1] three times, p1, k7.

Rows 12–13 establish stitch pattern.

**Row 14 (bead row):** P7, k1, [p1, k1] three times, k1, [PB, k2] twenty-five times, PB, k1, [p1, k1] three times, k1, p7.

Cont in patt, starting with a row 13, changing colors and placing bead rows as folls.

1 row patt.

Change to B

7 rows patt.

Change to A

3 rows patt.

Bead row.

1 row patt.

Change to B

2 rows patt.

Change to C

5 rows patt.

Change to A

3 rows patt.

Bead row.

1 row patt.

Change to B

4 rows patt.

Change to C

3 rows patt.

Change to A

3 rows patt.

Bead row.

1 row patt.

Change to C

2 rows patt.

**Row 54:** Bind/cast off 14 sts, ssk, k72, k2tog, k1, [p1, k1] three times, k1, p7. *(90 sts)*

**Row 55:** Bind/cast off 14 sts, p to end. *(76 sts)*

**Row 56:** Ssk, k72, k2tog. *(74 sts)*

Change to B

**Row 57:** Purl.

**Row 58:** Ssk, k70, k2tog. *(72 sts)*

**Row 59:** Purl.

Change to A

**Row 60:** Ssk, k68, k2tog. *(70 sts)*

**Row 61:** Purl.

**Row 62:** Knit

Bind/cast off.

## HANDLE

Using the cable method and A, cast on 11 sts.

**Row 1 (RS):** Knit

**Row 2:** Purl.

Rows 1–2 establish st st.

Work 6 more rows in st st.

**Row 9:** K5, PB, k5.

**Row 10:** Purl.

**Row 11:** Knit.

**Row 12:** Purl.

**Row 13:** K5, PB, k5.

Rows 10–13 establish 4-row bead patt.

Work 4-row bead patt eighteen more times.

**Row 86:** Purl.

**Row 87:** Knit

Rows 86–87 establish st st.

Work 6 more rows in st st.

**Row 94:** Purl.

Bind/cast off.

## FINISHING

Wrong-sides facing, fold the bag in half, aligning the top edges. Starting at the fold and using mattress stitch, sew up the sides. Turn under the rev st st section above the knit stitch fold line and slip stitch the row ends to the back of the first row of seed/moss stitch.

Right-sides facing, fold the handle in half lengthwise. Using mattress stitch, sew up the seam to make a tube for the handle. Fold the handle so that the beads are on the top. Sew the ends of the handle to the inside of the bag, aligning them with the side seams and the ends with the bottom of the rev st st section.

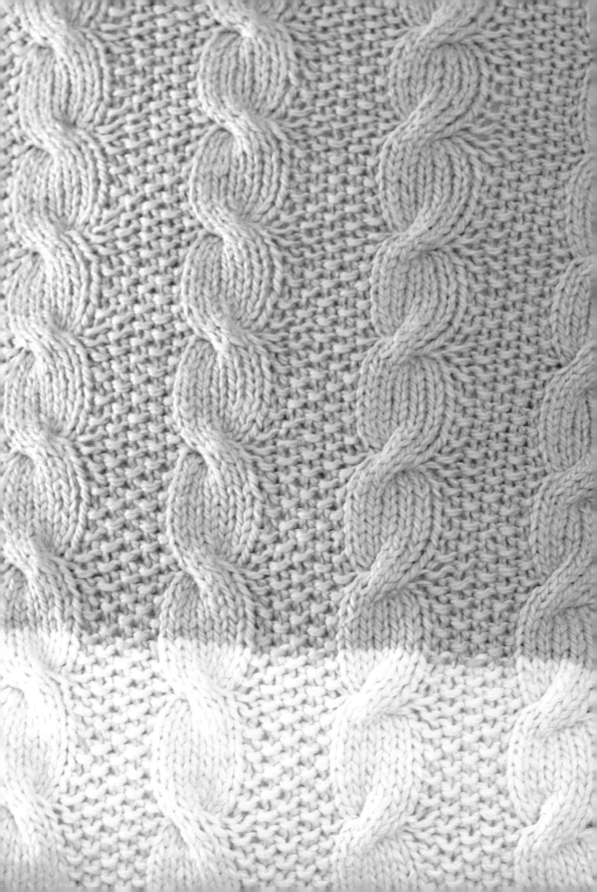

# keeping a knitting journal

The following journal pages have been especially designed for you to keep a record of each and every project you knit. There is space for a yarn sample, ball band, and information on the pattern, plus any additional notes.

There is nothing more frustrating than knitting a project you are proud of, having a friend admire it and request one, and being unable to fulfil that request because you can't find the magazine page the pattern came from, or because you substituted yarn and have no idea what you used. Worse still is if you cleverly made the pattern up, but can't find the envelope you wrote it on the back of.

Make this journal your own unique knitting record and not only will you be able to refer back to (and gloat proudly over) everything you have made, but you will also create a visual and written library that will motivate and inspire you for future knitting projects.

On the next page you will find a sample page filled in to give you an idea of how best to record your own knitting adventures.

# my project

**name:** Pull-on hat

**date begun:** 3 December

**date completed:** 10 December

**pattern source:** page 22, Knitting in no
Time, Melody Griffiths

**who I made it for:** Jackie's Christmas gift

**yarn:** Noro silk garden, shade 89

**needle size:** US 8/5mm

**project measurements:** 20³/₄in/53cm
around the brim

**gauge/tension**

**stitches per inch/centimeter:** 18

**rows per inch/centimeter:** 24

**my notes:** This was my first project on
double-pointed needles. Much easier than I
thought it would be. The hat also knitted up
quickly and I didn't have time to get bored
with it. There's a neat pattern trick where the
stitches between increases are the same as the
round number that made it really easy to
work out where I was; very clever.
The hat has already been admired by Lisa, so
I guess I'll be knitting another one, but I'm
going to try using a plain-colored yarn for
that one - Lisa likes pink.

# my project

name:

date begun:

date completed:

pattern source:

who I made it for:

yarn:

needle size:

project measurements:

my notes:

gauge/tension

stitches per inch/centimeter:

rows per inch/centimeter:

attach ball band
and/or yarn
sample here

attach
photograph of
project here

# my project

name:

date begun:

date completed:

pattern source:

who I made it for:

yarn:

needle size:

project measurements:

my notes:

gauge/tension

stitches per inch/centimeter:

rows per inch/centimeter:

attach ball band
and/or yarn
sample here

attach
photograph of
project here

# my project

name:

date begun:

date completed:

pattern source:

who I made it for:

yarn:

needle size:

project measurements:

my notes:

gauge/tension

stitches per inch/centimeter:

rows per inch/centimeter:

attach ball band
and/or yarn
sample here

attach
photograph of
project here

# my project

name:

date begun:

date completed:

pattern source:

who I made it for:

yarn:

needle size:

project measurements:

my notes:

gauge/tension

stitches per inch/centimeter:

rows per inch/centimeter:

attach ball band
and/or yarn
sample here

attach
photograph of
project here

# my project

name:

date begun:

date completed:

pattern source:

who I made it for:

yarn:

needle size:

project measurements:

my notes:

gauge/tension

stitches per inch/centimeter:

rows per inch/centimeter:

attach ball band
and/or yarn
sample here

attach
photograph of
project here

# my project

name:

date begun:

date completed:

pattern source:

who I made it for:

yarn:

needle size:

project measurements:

my notes:

gauge/tension

stitches per inch/centimeter:

rows per inch/centimeter:

attach ball band
and/or yarn
sample here

attach
photograph of
project here

# my project

name:

date begun:

date completed:

pattern source:


who I made it for:

yarn:


needle size:

project measurements:


my notes:

gauge/tension

stitches per inch/centimeter:

rows per inch/centimeter:

attach ball band
and/or yarn
sample here

attach
photograph of
project here

# my project

name:

date begun:

date completed:

pattern source:

who I made it for:

yarn:

needle size:

project measurements:

my notes:

gauge/tension

stitches per inch/centimeter:

rows per inch/centimeter:

attach ball band
and/or yarn
sample here

attach
photograph of
project here

# my project

name:

date begun:

date completed:

pattern source:

who I made it for:

yarn:

needle size:

project measurements:

my notes:

gauge/tension

stitches per inch/centimeter:

rows per inch/centimeter:

attach ball band
and/or yarn
sample here

attach
photograph of
project here

# my project

name: _____

date begun: _____

date completed: _____

pattern source: _____

who I made it for: _____

yarn: _____

needle size: _____

project measurements: _____

_____

_____

_____

my notes: _____

_____

_____

_____

_____

_____

_____

_____

_____

_____

_____

_____

_____

gauge/tension _____

stitches per inch/centimeter: _____

rows per inch/centimeter: _____

attach ball band
and/or yarn
sample here

attach
photograph of
project here

# my project

name:

date begun:

date completed:

pattern source:

who I made it for:

yarn:

needle size:

project measurements:

my notes:

gauge/tension

stitches per inch/centimeter:

rows per inch/centimeter:

attach ball band
and/or yarn
sample here

attach
photograph of
project here

# my project

name:

date begun:

date completed:

pattern source:


who I made it for:

yarn:


needle size:

project measurements:


my notes:

gauge/tension

stitches per inch/centimeter:

rows per inch/centimeter:

attach ball band
and/or yarn
sample here

attach
photograph of
project here

# my project

name:

date begun:

date completed:

pattern source:


who I made it for:

yarn:


needle size:

project measurements:


my notes:

gauge/tension

stitches per inch/centimeter:

rows per inch/centimeter:


attach ball band
and/or yarn
sample here


attach
photograph of
project here

# my project

name:

date begun:

date completed:

pattern source:

who I made it for:

yarn:

needle size:

project measurements:

my notes:

gauge/tension

stitches per inch/centimeter:

rows per inch/centimeter:

attach ball band
and/or yarn
sample here

attach
photograph of
project here

# my project

name:

date begun:

date completed:

pattern source:

who I made it for:

yarn:

needle size:

project measurements:

my notes:

gauge/tension

stitches per inch/centimeter:

rows per inch/centimeter:

attach ball band
and/or yarn
sample here

attach
photograph of
project here

# my project

name: ......................................................

date begun: ................................................

date completed: ............................................

pattern source: ............................................

who I made it for: .........................................

yarn: ......................................................

needle size: ...............................................

project measurements: ......................................

my notes: ..................................................

.......................................................................

.......................................................................

.......................................................................

.......................................................................

.......................................................................

.......................................................................

.......................................................................

.......................................................................

.......................................................................

.......................................................................

.......................................................................

gauge/tension ..............................................

stitches per inch/centimeter: ..............................

rows per inch/centimeter: ..................................

attach ball band
and/or yarn
sample here

attach
photograph of
project here

# my project

name:

date begun:

date completed:

pattern source:

who I made it for:

yarn:

needle size:

project measurements:

my notes:

gauge/tension

stitches per inch/centimeter:

rows per inch/centimeter:

attach ball band
and/or yarn
sample here

attach
photograph of
project here

# my project

name: _____

date begun: _____

date completed: _____

pattern source: _____

_____

who I made it for: _____

yarn: _____

_____

needle size: _____

project measurements: _____

_____

_____

_____

my notes: _____

_____

_____

_____

_____

_____

_____

_____

_____

_____

_____

_____

gauge/tension _____

stitches per inch/centimeter: _____

rows per inch/centimeter: _____

attach ball band
and/or yarn
sample here

attach
photograph of
project here

# my project

name:

date begun:

date completed:

pattern source:

who I made it for:

yarn:

needle size:

project measurements:

my notes:

gauge/tension

stitches per inch/centimeter:

rows per inch/centimeter:

attach ball band
and/or yarn
sample here

attach
photograph of
project here

# my project

name:

date begun:

date completed:

pattern source:


who I made it for:

yarn:


needle size:

project measurements:


my notes:

gauge/tension

stitches per inch/centimeter:

rows per inch/centimeter:

attach ball band
and/or yarn
sample here

attach
photograph of
project here

# my project

name:

date begun:

date completed:

pattern source:

who I made it for:

yarn:

needle size:

project measurements:

my notes:

gauge/tension

stitches per inch/centimeter:

rows per inch/centimeter:

attach ball band
and/or yarn
sample here

attach
photograph of
project here

# my project

name:

date begun:

date completed:

pattern source:

who I made it for:

yarn:

needle size:

project measurements:

my notes:

gauge/tension

stitches per inch/centimeter:

rows per inch/centimeter:

attach ball band
and/or yarn
sample here

attach
photograph of
project here

# my project

name:

date begun:

date completed:

pattern source:


who I made it for:

yarn:


needle size:

project measurements:


my notes:

gauge/tension

stitches per inch/centimeter:

rows per inch/centimeter:

attach ball band
and/or yarn
sample here

attach
photograph of
project here

# my project

name:

date begun:

date completed:

pattern source:

who I made it for:

yarn:

needle size:

project measurements:

my notes:

gauge/tension

stitches per inch/centimeter:

rows per inch/centimeter:

attach ball band
and/or yarn
sample here

attach
photograph of
project here

# my project

name:

date begun:

date completed:

pattern source:

who I made it for:

yarn:

needle size:

project measurements:

my notes:

gauge/tension

stitches per inch/centimeter:

rows per inch/centimeter:

attach ball band
and/or yarn
sample here

attach
photograph of
project here

# my project

name:

date begun:

date completed:

pattern source:


who I made it for:

yarn:


needle size:

project measurements:




my notes:

gauge/tension

stitches per inch/centimeter:

rows per inch/centimeter:

attach ball band
and/or yarn
sample here

attach
photograph of
project here

# *my project*

name:

date begun:

date completed:

pattern source:

who I made it for:

yarn:

needle size:

project measurements:

my notes:

gauge/tension

stitches per inch/centimeter:

rows per inch/centimeter:

attach ball band
and/or yarn
sample here

attach
photograph of
project here

# my project

name:

date begun:

date completed:

pattern source:

who I made it for:

yarn:

needle size:

project measurements:

my notes:

gauge/tension

stitches per inch/centimeter:

rows per inch/centimeter:

attach ball band
and/or yarn
sample here

attach
photograph of
project here

# my project

name:

date begun:

date completed:

pattern source:

who I made it for:

yarn:

needle size:

project measurements:

my notes:

gauge/tension

stitches per inch/centimeter:

rows per inch/centimeter:

attach ball band
and/or yarn
sample here

attach
photograph of
project here

# my project

name:

date begun:

date completed:

pattern source:

who I made it for:

yarn:

needle size:

project measurements:

my notes:

gauge/tension

stitches per inch/centimeter:

rows per inch/centimeter:

attach ball band
and/or yarn
sample here

attach
photograph of
project here

# *my project*

name:

date begun:

date completed:

pattern source:

who I made it for:

yarn:

needle size:

project measurements:

my notes:

gauge/tension

stitches per inch/centimeter:

rows per inch/centimeter:

attach ball band
and/or yarn
sample here

attach
photograph of
project here

# my project

name:

date begun:

date completed:

pattern source:

who I made it for:

yarn:

needle size:

project measurements:

my notes:

gauge/tension

stitches per inch/centimeter:

rows per inch/centimeter:

attach ball band
and/or yarn
sample here

attach
photograph of
project here

# my project

name:

date begun:

date completed:

pattern source:


who I made it for:

yarn:



needle size:

project measurements:




my notes:

gauge/tension

stitches per inch/centimeter:

rows per inch/centimeter:



attach ball band
and/or yarn
sample here




attach
photograph of
project here

# my project

name:

date begun:

date completed:

pattern source:


who I made it for:

yarn:


needle size:

project measurements:


my notes:

gauge/tension

stitches per inch/centimeter:

rows per inch/centimeter:

attach ball band
and/or yarn
sample here

attach
photograph of
project here

# my project

name:

date begun:

date completed:

pattern source:

who I made it for:

yarn:

needle size:

project measurements:

my notes:

gauge/tension

stitches per inch/centimeter:

rows per inch/centimeter:

attach ball band
and/or yarn
sample here

attach
photograph of
project here

# my project

name:

date begun:

date completed:

pattern source:


who I made it for:

yarn:


needle size:

project measurements:


my notes:

gauge/tension

stitches per inch/centimeter:

rows per inch/centimeter:

attach ball band
and/or yarn
sample here

attach
photograph of
project here

# my project

name:

date begun:

date completed:

pattern source:


who I made it for:

yarn:


needle size:

project measurements:




my notes:

gauge/tension

stitches per inch/centimeter:

rows per inch/centimeter:

attach ball band
and/or yarn
sample here

attach
photograph of
project here

# my project

name:

date begun:

date completed:

pattern source:


who I made it for:

yarn:


needle size:

project measurements:



my notes:

gauge/tension

stitches per inch/centimeter:

rows per inch/centimeter:

attach ball band
and/or yarn
sample here

attach
photograph of
project here

# my project

name:

date begun:

date completed:

pattern source:

who I made it for:

yarn:

needle size:

project measurements:

my notes:

gauge/tension

stitches per inch/centimeter:

rows per inch/centimeter:

attach ball band
and/or yarn
sample here

attach
photograph of
project here

# my project

name:

date begun:

date completed:

pattern source:

who I made it for:

yarn:

needle size:

project measurements:

my notes:

gauge/tension

stitches per inch/centimeter:

rows per inch/centimeter:

attach ball band
and/or yarn
sample here

attach
photograph of
project here

# my project

name:

date begun:

date completed:

pattern source:


who I made it for:

yarn:


needle size:

project measurements:


my notes:

gauge/tension

stitches per inch/centimeter:

rows per inch/centimeter:


attach ball band
and/or yarn
sample here


attach
photograph of
project here

# my project

name: ..................................................

date begun: ..........................................

date completed: ....................................

pattern source: ....................................
..................................................................

who I made it for: ................................

yarn: ....................................................
..................................................................
..................................................................

needle size: ........................................

project measurements: ......................
..................................................................
..................................................................
..................................................................

my notes: ............................................
..................................................................
..................................................................
..................................................................
..................................................................
..................................................................
..................................................................
..................................................................
..................................................................
..................................................................
..................................................................
..................................................................
..................................................................

gauge/tension ....................................

stitches per inch/centimeter: ..............

rows per inch/centimeter: ....................

attach ball band
and/or yarn
sample here

attach
photograph of
project here

# my project

name:

date begun:

date completed:

pattern source:

who I made it for:

yarn:

needle size:

project measurements:

my notes:

gauge/tension

stitches per inch/centimeter:

rows per inch/centimeter:

attach ball band
and/or yarn
sample here

attach
photograph of
project here

# my project

name:

date begun:

date completed:

pattern source:


who I made it for:

yarn:


needle size:

project measurements:


my notes:

gauge/tension

stitches per inch/centimeter:

rows per inch/centimeter:

attach ball band
and/or yarn
sample here

attach
photograph of
project here

# my project

name:

date begun:

date completed:

pattern source:

who I made it for:

yarn:

needle size:

project measurements:

my notes:

gauge/tension

stitches per inch/centimeter:

rows per inch/centimeter:

attach ball band
and/or yarn
sample here

attach
photograph of
project here

# my project

name:

date begun:

date completed:

pattern source:


who I made it for:

yarn:


needle size:

project measurements:


my notes:

gauge/tension

stitches per inch/centimeter:

rows per inch/centimeter:

attach ball band
and/or yarn
sample here

attach
photograph of
project here

# my project

name:

date begun:

date completed:

pattern source:

who I made it for:

yarn:

needle size:

project measurements:

my notes:

gauge/tension

stitches per inch/centimeter:

rows per inch/centimeter:

attach ball band
and/or yarn
sample here

attach
photograph of
project here

# my project

name:

date begun:

date completed:

pattern source:

who I made it for:

yarn:

needle size:

project measurements:

my notes:

gauge/tension

stitches per inch/centimeter:

rows per inch/centimeter:

attach ball band
and/or yarn
sample here

attach
photograph of
project here

# my project

name:

date begun:

date completed:

pattern source:

who I made it for:

yarn:

needle size:

project measurements:

my notes:

gauge/tension

stitches per inch/centimeter:

rows per inch/centimeter:

attach ball band
and/or yarn
sample here

attach
photograph of
project here

# my project

name:

date begun:

date completed:

pattern source:

who I made it for:

yarn:

needle size:

project measurements:

my notes:

gauge/tension

stitches per inch/centimeter:

rows per inch/centimeter:

attach ball band
and/or yarn
sample here

attach
photograph of
project here

# my project

name:

date begun:

date completed:

pattern source:


who I made it for:

yarn:


needle size:

project measurements:




my notes:

gauge/tension

stitches per inch/centimeter:

rows per inch/centimeter:




attach ball band
and/or yarn
sample here




attach
photograph of
project here

# my project

name:

date begun:

date completed:

pattern source:


who I made it for:

yarn:


needle size:

project measurements:


my notes:

gauge/tension

stitches per inch/centimeter:

rows per inch/centimeter:

attach ball band
and/or yarn
sample here

attach
photograph of
project here

# my project

name:

date begun:

date completed:

pattern source:

who I made it for:

yarn:

needle size:

project measurements:

my notes:

gauge/tension

stitches per inch/centimeter:

rows per inch/centimeter:

attach ball band
and/or yarn
sample here

attach
photograph of
project here

# my project

name:

date begun:

date completed:

pattern source:

who I made it for:

yarn:

needle size:

project measurements:

my notes:

gauge/tension

stitches per inch/centimeter:

rows per inch/centimeter:

attach ball band
and/or yarn
sample here

attach
photograph of
project here

# my project

name:

date begun:

date completed:

pattern source:

who I made it for:

yarn:

needle size:

project measurements:

my notes:

gauge/tension

stitches per inch/centimeter:

rows per inch/centimeter:

attach ball band
and/or yarn
sample here

attach
photograph of
project here

# my project

name:

date begun:

date completed:

pattern source:


who I made it for:

yarn:


needle size:

project measurements:


my notes:

gauge/tension

stitches per inch/centimeter:

rows per inch/centimeter:


attach ball band
and/or yarn
sample here


attach
photograph of
project here

# my project

name:

date begun:

date completed:

pattern source:

who I made it for:

yarn:

needle size:

project measurements:

my notes:

gauge/tension

stitches per inch/centimeter:

rows per inch/centimeter:

attach ball band
and/or yarn
sample here

attach
photograph of
project here

# my project

name:

date begun:

date completed:

pattern source:


who I made it for:

yarn:


needle size:

project measurements:


my notes:

gauge/tension

stitches per inch/centimeter:

rows per inch/centimeter:

attach ball band
and/or yarn
sample here

attach
photograph of
project here

# my project

name:

date begun:

date completed:

pattern source:

who I made it for:

yarn:

needle size:

project measurements:

my notes:

gauge/tension

stitches per inch/centimeter:

rows per inch/centimeter:

attach ball band
and/or yarn
sample here

attach
photograph of
project here

# my project

name:

date begun:

date completed:

pattern source:


who I made it for:

yarn:


needle size:

project measurements:


my notes:

gauge/tension

stitches per inch/centimeter:

rows per inch/centimeter:

attach ball band
and/or yarn
sample here

attach
photograph of
project here

# my project

name:

date begun:

date completed:

pattern source:

who I made it for:

yarn:

needle size:

project measurements:

my notes:

gauge/tension

stitches per inch/centimeter:

rows per inch/centimeter:

attach ball band
and/or yarn
sample here

attach
photograph of
project here

# my project

name:

date begun:

date completed:

pattern source:

who I made it for:

yarn:

needle size:

project measurements:

my notes:

gauge/tension

stitches per inch/centimeter:

rows per inch/centimeter:

attach ball band
and/or yarn
sample here

attach
photograph of
project here

# my project

name:

date begun:

date completed:

pattern source:


who I made it for:

yarn:


needle size:

project measurements:


my notes:

gauge/tension

stitches per inch/centimeter:

rows per inch/centimeter:


attach ball band
and/or yarn
sample here


attach
photograph of
project here

# my project

name:

date begun:

date completed:

pattern source:

who I made it for:

yarn:

needle size:

project measurements:

my notes:

gauge/tension

stitches per inch/centimeter:

rows per inch/centimeter:

attach ball band
and/or yarn
sample here

attach
photograph of
project here

# my project

name:

date begun:

date completed:

pattern source:

who I made it for:

yarn:

needle size:

project measurements:

my notes:

gauge/tension

stitches per inch/centimeter:

rows per inch/centimeter:

attach ball band
and/or yarn
sample here

attach
photograph of
project here

# my project

name:

date begun:

date completed:

pattern source:


who I made it for:

yarn:


needle size:

project measurements:


my notes:

gauge/tension

stitches per inch/centimeter:

rows per inch/centimeter:

attach ball band
and/or yarn
sample here

attach
photograph of
project here

# my project

name:

date begun:

date completed:

pattern source:

who I made it for:

yarn:

needle size:

project measurements:

my notes:

gauge/tension

stitches per inch/centimeter:

rows per inch/centimeter:

attach ball band
and/or yarn
sample here

attach
photograph of
project here

# *designing knitwear*

Simple projects that don't require an accurate fit are easy to design.
Here are the steps to follow to make and knit your own scarf.

Decide how long and wide the scarf will be (here, it will be 10in/25cm wide and 40in/100cm long) and the stitch pattern you will use. Do you want to include any color work or beading? Once you have made these decisions, visit your yarn store.

Buy one ball of your chosen yarn. Also buy small amounts of any embellishments you want to use. At home, with the yarn in front of you, refine your design ideas. These may change once you have knitted a swatch, but you do need a starting point.

Knit your swatch, following this procedure. Weigh the ball/s of yarn before you start. Check the tension on the ball band and cast on ten more stitches than the number stated. Knit ten more rows than stated, then bind/cast off. Put all elements of your design into the swatch. Knit it in your chosen stitch pattern. If there is a motif, knit it in and add any beading or cables.

Once you have finished swatching, weigh the left-over yarn. Weigh each ball separately and deduct this figure from the original weight to establish how much of each yarn you used. Record these weights carefully.

Now measure your swatch to find out your tension (see page 18). Here, it is 18 stitches and 24 rows to 4in/10cm. Do the following sums:

10in/25cm (scarf width) ÷ 4in/10cm
  (swatch width) = 2.5

18 (stitches in swatch) x 2.5 = 45
  (width of scarf in stitches)

40in/100cm (scarf length) ÷ 4in/10cm
  (swatch length) = 10

24 (rows in swatch) x 10 = 240
  (length of scarf in rows)

Now you need to work out how much yarn you will need to knit the scarf. The easiest way is to first work out the number of stitches in the swatch and the number in the scarf, though the number may be scary!

18 x 24 = 432 (stitches in measured area of swatch)
45 x 240 = 10,800 (stitches in scarf)

Now work out how many swatches you would have to knit in order to knit the scarf.

108,000 (stitches in scarf) ÷ 432 (stitches in swatch) = 25

Multiply the weight of yarn used in your swatch, 0.7oz/19g in this example, by this figure to find out how much yarn to buy.

0.7/19 x 25 = 17.5oz/475g

If the yarn is sold in 1¾oz/50g balls, this is ten balls. However, you weighed the whole swatch, but actually knitted about 100 more stitches than we have counted (your swatch was roughly 10 stitches and 10 rows larger than the measured area). 100 stitches is almost a quarter of the swatch, so you need buy only eight balls of yarn.

If you have used more than one color yarn, you need to work out how much of each color to buy. For example, if you have knitted a pink heart motif that used 0.14oz/4g of yarn and want 14 of them on the scarf, this is the sum:

0.14oz/4g (weight of pink yarn for 1 heart) x 14 = 1.96oz/56g

One ball, plus the remainder of the ball you swatched with, will therefore be ample.

# writing patterns

When you design your first project you will also write your first pattern. Do this well and you will be able to re-knit it whenever you like. Here are some sound tips and advice on writing great patterns.

The secrets of good pattern writing are clarity and consistency. If every stitch is included and the pattern is logical, then you, and others, will be able to knit them easily. Imagine the pleasure in having your scarf admired and being able to offer the admirer a pattern to knit it from, confident that that pattern is perfect.

Firstly, look through some pattern books and choose a style you find easy to follow. Spend some time analysing it and writing notes. Are the instructions capitalized or in lower case letters? How are the rows indicated? Which abbreviations are used? How are repeats indicated? How are stitch counts shown? When you have worked through the pattern, write up your own pattern style sheet. This will be your guide to all the patterns you write, so put in as much information as possible. Remember that this is YOUR style sheet, so you can change any styles you didn't like in the original pattern.

The best way to construct your pattern is to do a rough draft, which you can do from your stitch and row calculations and your initial design ideas (see page 139). Type this out, making the lines double-spaced, and print it. Start knitting and, as you work, write in any information that is missing. Write it in full, don't jot down a note and hope that later you remember what it meant.

If your print-out becomes covered in scribbles, stop knitting and go and type in all the information you have so far and print it out again.

Once you have finished your knitting, write the pattern out in full and do a fresh print out. Now go through it carefully, checking the following:

**Materials:** include the name and color of the yarn/s, the number of balls of each yarn needed, and the needle size/s used, plus any other materials needed.

**Size:** measure the finished project and note these measurements.

**Tension:** this will be the tension from your swatch, but check it again on the actual project.

**Abbreviations:** use a standard list (see page 20) but write out any special abbreviations in full on your pattern.

**Cast on:** specify yarn color and needle size if there are more than one of each.

**Rows:** the first row should say whether this is the right or wrong side of the work. Make sure each row is numbered and that the numbers run consecutively. If you have to knit a measured length rather than a number of rows, you can say "Next row" rather than a row number, but it is helpful to number as many rows as possible.

**Color and needle changes:** make sure these are indicated in the right places.

**Stitch counts:** count the number of stitches in every written-out row. If there is shaping, put a stitch count at the end of each increase or decrease row.

If you are going to give the pattern to others to knit and you want to be sure it is right, knit it again from your own instructions. Don't make any assumptions, just knit what you have written and you will soon see if you have made any mistakes in the pattern.

This may all sound rather time-consuming, but this is how the professionals do their patterns and if the result is a perfect pattern, then your time has been well spent.

140

# knitter's graph paper

The graph paper on these pages is specially designed for knitters, with each square being the proportions of a single stitch. Design your motifs on this paper and they will knit up just as they were drawn.

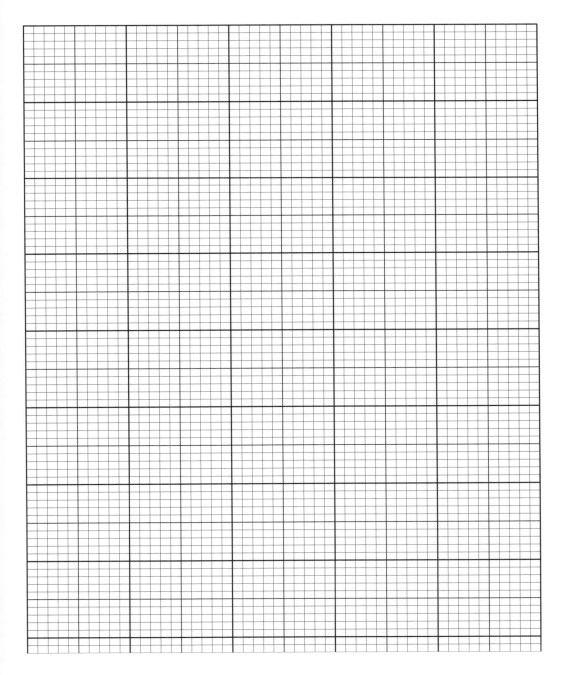

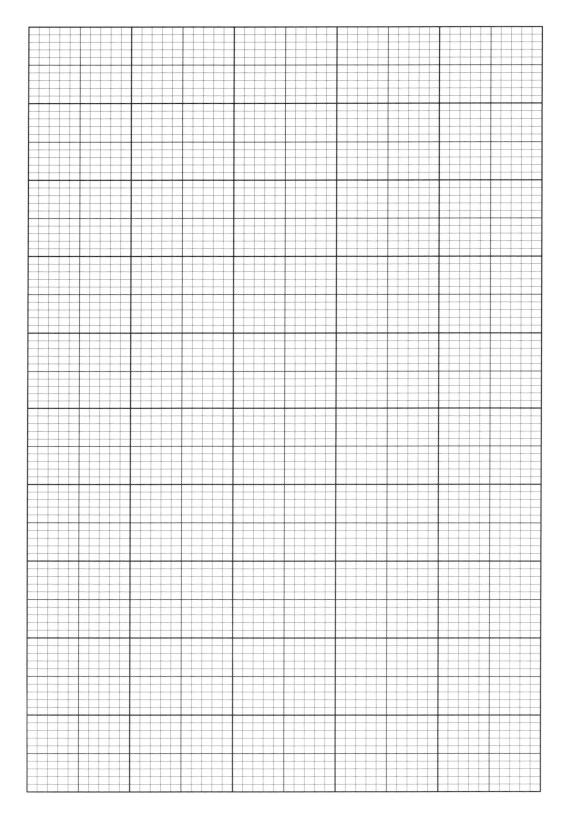

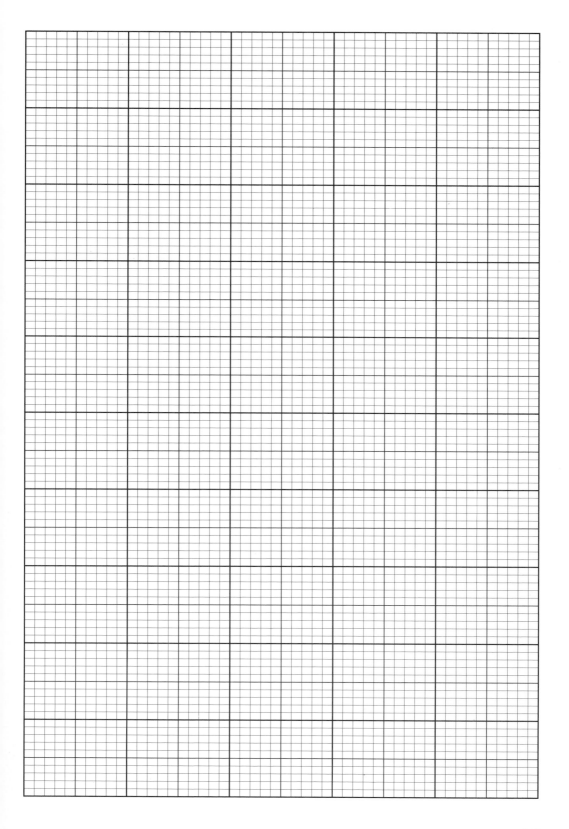

Published in 2007 by
CICO Books an imprint of
Ryland Peters & Small Ltd
20–21 Jockey's Fields
London WC1R 4BW

519 Broadway, 5th Floor
New York NY10012
www.rylandpeters.com

10 9 8 7 6 5 4 3 2 1

A CIP catalog record for this book is
available from the British Library and
Library of Congress.

ISBN 10: 1 904991 97 1
ISBN 13: 978 1 904991 97 7


Printed in China

Contributing writer and editor: Kate Haxell
Design: Roger Hammond
Photography: Matthew Dickens (unless
otherwise credited)

**Picture Credits**
Tino Tedaldi: page 70.
Sandra Lousada: front cover from Cotton
Knits by Debbie Bliss. Bag designed by
Debbie Bliss.